Editor
Eric Migliaccio

Managing Editor
Ina Massler Levin, M.A.

Illustrator
Clint McKnight

Cover Artist
Brenda DiAntonis

Art Production Manager
Kevin Barnes

Imaging
Craig Gunnell

Publisher
Mary D. Smith, M.S. Ed.

NONFICTION READING COMPREHENSION

Social Studies

Grade 4

Ideal for Test Practice

Includes Standards & Benchmarks

Author

Ruth Foster, M.Ed.

Teacher Created Resources, Inc.
6421 Industry Way
Westminster, CA 92683
www.teachercreated.com

ISBN: 978-1-4206-8025-6

©2006 Teacher Created Resources, Inc.
Reprinted, 2010
Made in U.S.A.

Table of Contents

Introduction

* **Social studies is thrilling**.

  Think of the countless number of children saved by the heroic effort of bringing diphtheria medicine to Nome, Alaska, by dogsled in 1925 in blizzard conditions.

* **It has changed our world.**

  Think of how Elizabeth Stanton worked for women's right to vote.

* **It affects our lives daily.**

  Think of how we use our interstate highway system and how it is numbered.

Reading comprehension can be practiced and improved while coupled with social studies instruction. This book presents short, fascinating stories that focus on social studies topics. The stories were chosen to arouse curiosity; augment basic social studies facts taught at this grade level; and introduce a world of ideas, people, and events.

A page of questions follows each story. These questions will make students familiar with different types of test questions. In addition, the practice they provide will help students develop good testing skills. Questions are written so that they lead the reader to focus on what was read. They provide practice for finding the main idea, as well as specific details. They provide practice in deciphering new and unknown vocabulary words. In addition, the questions encourage students to think beyond the facts. For example, every question set has an analogy question where students are expected to think about the relationship between two things and find a pair of words with the same type of relationship. Other questions provide an opportunity for students to infer and consider possible consequences relevant to the information provided in the story.

The book is designed so that writing can be incorporated into every lesson. The level of writing will depend on what the teacher desires, as well as the needs of the students.

Lessons in *Nonfiction Reading Comprehension: Social Studies, Grade 4* meet and are correlated to the Mid-continent Research for Education and Learning (McREL) standards. They are listed on page 8.

A place for *Nonfiction Reading Comprehension: Social Studies, Grade 4* can be found in every classroom or home. It can be a part of daily instruction in time designated for both reading and social studies. It can be used for both group and individual instruction. Stories can be read with someone or on one's own. *Nonfiction Reading Comprehension: Social Studies, Grade 4* can help students improve in a multitude of areas, including reading, social studies, critical thinking, writing, and test taking.

Using This Book

The Stories

Each story in *Nonfiction Reading Comprehension: Social Studies, Grade 4* is a separate unit. For this reason, the stories can be (but do not have to be) read in order. A teacher can choose any story that matches classroom activity.

Stories can be assigned to be read during social studies or reading periods. They can be used as classroom work or as supplemental material.

Each story is five paragraphs long and ranges from 325–350 words in length. They are written at the fourth-grade level and have elementary sentence structure.

New Words

Each story includes a list of eight new words. Each of the new words is used a minimum of two times in the story. New words may sometimes have an addition of a simple word ending, such as *s, ed,* or *ing*. The new words are introduced in the story in the same order that they are presented in the new word list. Many of the new words are found in more than one story. Mastery of the new words may not come immediately, but practice articulating, seeing, and writing the words will build a foundation for future learning.

* A teacher may choose to have the children read and repeat the words together as a class.

* While it is true that the majority of the words are defined explicitly or in context in the stories, a teacher may choose to discuss and define the new words before the children begin reading. This will improve and reinforce sight-word identification and reading vocabulary.

* A teacher may present the class with two sentences that contain the new word. Only one sentence, however, will use the word correctly. Children will be asked to identify which sentence is correct. For example, for the word *inhospitable*, the teacher might say,

   "We were not offered food or shelter, as the people were very inhospitable."

   "The inhospitable people kindly welcomed us with open arms."

* A teacher may also allow children to choose one new word to add to their weekly spelling list. This provides children with an opportunity to feel they are a part of a decision-making process, as well as gain "ownership" of new words.

* A teacher may choose to have children go through the story after it is read and circle each new word one or two times.

Using This Book

The Writing Link

A teacher may choose to link writing exercises to the social studies stories presented in the book. All writing links reinforce handwriting and spelling skills. Writing links with optional sentence tasks reinforce sentence construction and punctuation.

* A teacher may choose to have a child pick one new word from the list of new words and write it out. Space for the word write-out is provided in this book. This option may seem simple, but it provides a child with an opportunity to take control. The child is not overwhelmed by the task of the word write-out because the child is choosing the word. It also reinforces sight-word identification. If a teacher has begun to instruct children in cursive writing, the teacher can ask the child to write out the word twice, once in print and once in cursive.

* A teacher may choose to have a child write out a complete sentence using one of the new words. The sentences can by formulated together as a class or as individual work. Depending on other classroom work, the teacher may want to remind children about capital letters and ending punctuation.

* A teacher may require a child to write out a sentence after the story questions have been answered. The sentence may or may not contain a new word. The sentence may have one of the following starts:

  - I learned . . .
  - I thought . . .

  - Did you know . . .
  - An interesting thing about . . .

If the teacher decides on this type of sentence formation, the teacher may want to show children how they can use words directly from the story to help form their sentences, as well as make sure that words in their sentences are not misspelled. For example, for the first paragraph in the selection titled "Dog Boots" (page 10), possible sample sentence write-outs are . . .

"I learned that the Inuit live in the far north."

"I thought the Arctic was an inhospitable place to live, but it is not."

"Did you know that the Inuit were once known as Eskimos?"

"An interesting thing about the Inuit is that they live in the Arctic areas of Alaska and Canada, as well as Greenland and Siberia."

This type of exercise reinforces spelling and sentence structure. It also teaches a child responsibility: a child learns to go back to the story to check word spelling. It also provides elementary report-writing skills. Students are taking information in a story source and reporting it in their own sentence construction.

The Questions

Five questions follow every story. Questions always contain one main-idea, one specific-detail, and one analogy question.

* The main-idea question pushes a child to focus on the topic of what was read. It allows practice in discerning between answers that are too broad or too narrow.

* The specific-detail question requires a child to retrieve or recall a particular fact mentioned in the story. Children gain practice referring back to a source. They also are pushed to think about the structure of the story. Where would this fact most likely be mentioned in the story? Which paragraph would most likely contain the fact they are retrieving?

* The analogy question pushes a child to develop reasoning skills. It pairs two words mentioned in the story and asks the child to think about how the words relate to each other. A child is then asked to find an analogous pair. Children are expected to recognize and use analogies in all course readings, written work, and in listening. This particular type of question is found on many cognitive-functioning tests.

The remaining two questions are a mixture of vocabulary, identifying what is true or not true, sequencing, or inference questions. Going back and reading the word in context can always answer vocabulary questions. The inference questions are the most difficult for many students, but they provide practice for what students will find on standardized tests. They also encourage students to think beyond the story and to think critically about how facts can be interpreted or why something works.

The Test Link

Standardized tests have become obligatory in schools throughout our nation and the world. There are certain test-taking skills and strategies that can be developed by using this resource.

* Students can answer the questions on the page by filling in the circle of the correct answer, or one may choose to have one's students use the answer sheet located at the back of the book (page 141). Filling in the bubble page provides practice responding in a standardized-test format.

* Questions are presented in a mixed-up order, though the main idea question is always placed in the numbers one, two, or three slot. The analogy question is always placed in the three, four, or five slots. This mixed-up order provides practice with standardized-test formats, where reading comprehension passages often have main-idea questions, but these type of questions are not necessarily placed first.

The Test Link (cont.)

✳ A teacher may want to point out to students that often a main-idea question can be used to help a child focus on what the story is about. A teacher may also want to point out that an analogy question can be done any time, as it is not crucial to the main focus of the story.

✳ A teacher may want to remind students to read every answer choice. Many children are afraid of not remembering information. Reinforcing this tip helps a child to remember that on multiple-choice tests, one is *identifying* the best answer, not making up an answer.

✳ A teacher may choose to discuss the strategy of eliminating wrong answer choices to find the correct one. Teachers should instruct children that even if they can eliminate only one answer choice, their guess has a better chance of being right. A teacher may want to go through several questions to demonstrate this strategy. For example, in the "Dog Boots" selection, there is the following question:

---

3. Why were holes cut in the dog boots?

   ⓐ so the dogs would not slip

   ⓑ so the dogs' paws could stay warm

   ⓒ so the dogs' paws would not soften

   ⓓ so the dogs would not get cut on the ice

A child may not be able to recall off the top of his or her head exactly why holes were cut in the dog boots, but after reading the answer choices, he or she may be able to eliminate wrong answer choices. For example, he or she may know that boots with holes cut out would not keep one as warm as boots without holes—so answer choice "b" is incorrect and can be eliminated. The same type of reasoning can be used to eliminate answer choice "d" (Boots with holes would allow contact with ice.) If contact from ice caused cuts, then boots with holes would not protect a dog from ice cuts. At this point, with two choices eliminated, even if a student guesses, he or she has a 50% chance of getting the correct answer. A teacher can remind students, too, that there is the option of going back and finding the paragraph where the holes in the dog boots are mentioned (paragraph 4).

The Thrill of Social Studies

The challenge in writing this book was to allow a child access to the thrills of social studies while understanding that many social-studies words and concepts are beyond a child's elementary grade level. It is hoped that the range of stories and the ways concepts are presented reinforces basic social-studies concepts, all while improving basic reading-comprehension skills. It is also hoped that a child's imagination is whetted. After reading each story, a child will want to question and find out more.

Meeting Standards

Listed below are the McREL standards for Language Arts Level 2 (Grades 3–5). All standards and benchmarks are used with permission from McREL.

Copyright 2004 McREL

Mid-continent Research for Education and Learning

4601 DTC Boulevard, Suite 500

Denver, CO 80237-2596

Telephone: (303) 337-0990

Website: www.mcrel.org/standards-benchmarks

McREL Standards are in **bold**. Benchmarks are in regular print. All lessons meet the following standards and benchmarks (unless noted).

Uses the stylistic and rhetorical aspects of writing

- Uses a variety of sentence structures in writing (All lessons where writing a complete sentence option is followed.)

Uses grammatical and mechanical conventions in written compositions

- Writes in cursive (All lessons where teacher follows the option of writing a sentence using a new word or completion of beginning sentence options in cursive.)
- Uses conventions of spelling, capitalization, and punctuation in writing compositions (All lessons where teacher follows option of writing a sentence using a new word or completion of beginning sentence options.)

Uses the general skills and strategies of the reading process

- Previews text
- Establishes a purpose for reading
- Represents concrete information as explicit mental pictures
- Uses phonetic and structural analysis techniques, syntactic structure, and semantic context to decode unknown words
- Use a variety of context clues to decode unknown words
- Understands level-appropriate reading vocabulary
- Monitors own reading strategies and makes modifications as needed
- Adjusts speed of reading to suit purpose and difficulty of material
- Understands the author's purpose

Uses reading skills and strategies to understand a variety of informational texts

- Uses reading skills and strategies to understand a variety of informational texts
- Summarizes and paraphrases information in texts
- Uses prior knowledge and experience to understand and respond to new information

Dog Boots

These are new words to practice.

Say each word 10 times.

* Arctic	* claws
* inhospitable	* dangle
* extremely	* injury
* survive	* thaw

Before or after reading the story, write one sentence that contains at least one new word.

_____

_____

_____

Dog Boots

The Inuit live in the far north. They live in the Arctic areas of Alaska, Canada, Greenland, and Siberia. For many years, the Inuit were known as Eskimos. To many people, the Arctic can be an inhospitable place to live. When something is inhospitable, it is not kind or welcoming. It is not hospitable.

Why can the Arctic seem inhospitable? It is covered in snow and ice and extremely, or very, cold. To the Inuit people, the Arctic is not inhospitable. The Inuit have learned to survive in the extremely cold world of snow and ice. The Inuit have learned to travel by sled. They use dogs to pull their sleds over the snow and ice. Using dogs helps the Inuit travel and survive in the cold Arctic.

The Inuit take very good care of their dogs. The dogs can keep themselves warm with their thick fur coats. At night, the dogs can stay warm by curling up into tight balls. They wrap their fluffy tails over their feet and noses. The Inuit don't need to worry about keeping the dogs warm, but they do have to do something to help. Sometimes, they make boots for their sled dogs. What kind of boots do the Inuit make for their dogs? When do they put the boots on?

The Inuit make the boots from bits of oilskin or canvas. Holes are cut in the front of the boots. The holes are for the dogs' front claws. With holes for the claws, the dogs could still grip. They could hold fast to the snowy ground and not slip while pulling a sled.

The boots are used to protect the dogs from serious injury, or harm, when the sea ice begins to thaw, or melt. The sea ice begins to thaw in the summer. Running on the wet ice softens the dogs' paws. To make matters worse, sharp needles of ice form on the ice's surface as it begins to melt. The sharp needles of ice could easily cut the dogs' softened paws and cause serious injury. The boots protect the dogs' feet from getting cut.

Dog Boots

After reading the story, answer the questions.
Fill in the circle next to the correct answer.

1. This story is mainly about
   a) where the Inuit live
   b) how sled dogs stay warm
   c) the Inuit and a kind of boot
   d) how the Inuit survive the cold

2. Which place listed below is one of the places where there are Inuit?
   a) Alaska
   b) Alabama
   c) Arizona
   d) Arkansas

3. Why are holes cut in the dog boots?
   a) so the dogs would not slip
   b) so the dogs' paws could stay warm
   c) so the dogs' paws would not soften
   d) so the dogs would not get cut on the ice

4. Think about how the word *inhospitable* relates to *welcoming*. What words relate in the same way?

   inhospitable : welcoming

   a) grip : hold
   b) soft : hard
   c) thaw : melt
   d) hospitable : kind

5. From the story, you can tell that
   a) sled dogs have longer claws than other dogs
   b) the Inuit people do not care about their dogs
   c) serious injury happens all the time in the Arctic
   d) the Arctic summer is warmer than the Arctic winter

Why They Had Wands

These are new words to practice.

Say each word 10 times.

✻ latter	✻ style
✻ wands	✻ headdresses
✻ dainty	✻ decorated
✻ delicate	✻ vermin

Before or after reading the story, write one sentence that contains at least one new word.

_____

_____

_____

Why They Had Wands

During the latter part (nearer the end) of the 1700s, many French women carried wands. The wands were dainty. When something is dainty, it is pretty or lovely in a delicate way. Why did the women during the latter 1700s carry dainty wands? What were the pretty and delicate wands for?

In the latter part of the 1700s, it was the style for French women to wear their hair up in high, towering headdresses. The headdresses were so high that the women had to duck when they went through doors. They were so high that carriage roofs had to be made higher! The towering headdresses even changed the way women slept. Women had to sleep sitting up. Sitting up kept the headdresses from harm.

It took hours to style one's hair. It also cost a lot of money. First, one had to make one's own hair fuller. To make one's own hair fuller, one used switches of false hair. Second, one brushed the switches and one's own hair over a framework. The framework was made of three things. It was made of wire, cotton padding, and cushions of horsehair. Third, the hair was coated with sticky cream. The sticky cream kept the hair in place.

Then, the hair was powdered. It was powdered with starch or wheat flour. (Starch is a white food substance found in potatoes and grains.) The powder was white or tinted pale colors. Lastly, the hair was decorated. It was decorated with strings of pearl, flowers, and feathers. The headdresses lasted for weeks— and this led to the reason why the women needed wands.

The women used the wands to scratch their heads. A woman could slide her wand into her hair to scratch her head and not harm her headdress. Why did the women need to scratch their heads? Lice and vermin! The lice and vermin lived in the headdresses. Lice are tiny insects that suck blood from people's scalps. Vermin are tiny pests like bugs and mice. It's a good thing our hair is not styled this way today!

Why They Had Wands

After reading the story, answer the questions.
Fill in the circle next to the correct answer.

1. What year would be in the latter part of the 1700s?

   (a) 1710

   (b) 1730

   (c) 1750

   (d) 1770

2. This story is mainly about

   (a) French women

   (b) big and little wands

   (c) a hairstyle from the past

   (d) where lice and vermin live

3. What was the fourth step in making a towering headdress?

   (a) brushing the hair onto a framework

   (b) coating the hair with a sticky cream

   (c) powdering the hair with flour or starch

   (d) decorating the hair with pearls, flowers, and feathers

4. Which word best fits in the blank? "That old house is not empty. It is filled with _____."

   (a) hair

   (b) lice

   (c) wands

   (d) vermin

5. Think about how the word *carriage* relates to *ride*. What words relate in the same way?

carriage : ride

   (a) lice : hair

   (b) wand : scratch

   (c) powder : cream

   (d) feather : headdress

Reading with One's Fingers

These are new words to practice.

Say each word 10 times.

✳ Braille	✳ alphabet
✳ concentrated	✳ cell
✳ scholarship	✳ raised
✳ ingenious	✳ banned

Before or after reading the story, write one sentence that contains at least one new word.

_____

_____

_____

Reading with One's Fingers

When Louis Braille went to school, he listened carefully. All the students took notes, but Braille just concentrated. He concentrated on memorizing what he heard. While other students worked out math problems on paper, Braille concentrated on working out the problems in his head. But there were times when Braille did not work. The other students worked. Braille just sat.

Braille, born in 1809, was blind. He could not see. Still, Braille wanted to learn. He did not want to just sit while other students read. He wanted books to read. He wanted books for the blind. Braille was given a scholarship. A scholarship is a gift of money to help a student go to school. Braille's scholarship was to a school for the blind.

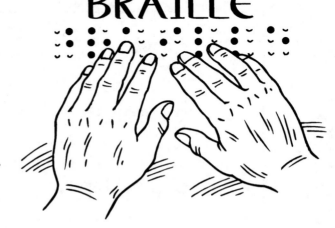

Braille hoped that his school would have books for him to read, but it did not. The school had only a few books with embossed, or raised, print. The books were big, expensive, and difficult to read because only a few sentences could fit on each page. Wanting a better way to read, Braille invented an ingenious alphabet. When something is ingenious, it is made or done in a clever way.

Braille's ingenious alphabet was based on cells. Each of Braille's cells had six dots, two across and three down. Some dots were raised. Others were lowered. Each letter of the alphabet had a set pattern of raised and lowered dots within a cell. Each cell was just the right size to fit within the tip of a finger. A person read by feeling the raised and lowered dots.

When Braille first invented his alphabet, some people banned it! When something is banned, it is not allowed. But students liked it so much that they used it in secret. Then, when people from the government first heard a blind person reading out loud a book printed in Braille, they thought it was a trick. It was not a trick. Braille was just an ingenious way for people to read with ones fingers. Today, books, magazines, and newspapers are printed in Braille all around the world.

Reading with One's Fingers

After reading the story, answer the questions.
Fill in the circle next to the correct answer.

1. Each of Braille's cells has how many dots?

   ⓐ 2

   ⓑ 3

   ⓒ 5

   ⓓ 6

2. What might be one reason the alphabet was banned?

   ⓐ Schools had spent lots of money on the old, expensive books.

   ⓑ Students would listen carefully and memorize what they had heard.

   ⓒ Students who were blind would not be able to read the Braille books.

   ⓓ The government did not think that a blind person could invent an ingenious alphabet.

3. This story is mainly about

   ⓐ Braille and school

   ⓑ Braille and fingertips

   ⓒ Braille and being blind

   ⓓ Braille and his alphabet

4. From the story, you can tell that the old embossed print

   ⓐ was very small

   ⓑ was very large

   ⓒ was hard to see

   ⓓ was hard to feel

5. Think about how the word *raise* relates to *lower*. What words relate in the same way?

raise : lower

   ⓐ ban : allow

   ⓑ read : book

   ⓒ alphabet : letter

   ⓓ school : scholarship

Jack and the Two-Headed Giant

These are new words to practice.

Say each word 10 times.

* anthropologist

* customs

* horrible

* enormous

* pouch

* squeeze

* astounded

* whey

Before or after reading the story, write one sentence that contains at least one new word.

_____

_____

_____

Jack and the Two-Headed Giant

What is an anthropologist? An anthropologist is a scientist who studies mankind. Some anthropologists study customs. A custom is something that has been done for a long time. A custom is a regular thing to do. Some customs involve storytelling. Anthropologists who study storytelling write down folk tales. They see where the tales are told and find out where the tales are from.

The first English settlers in the mountains of North Carolina told folk tales about a boy named Jack. The stories were passed from one storyteller to another. One story is about Jack and a two-headed giant. The story goes like this:

The King gave Jack a job clearing land. There was a problem with the job. The problem was a terrible, horrible, two-headed giant. With its two enormous mouths and terrible teeth, the giant liked nothing better than to feast on two children at the same time. This terrible, horrible giant lived on the land Jack needed to clear.

The King gave Jack some big hunks of cheese. Jack put the cheese in an enormous pouch under his jacket. Then, Jack took off to clear the land. Soon, he met the giant. Jack was afraid, but he did not let the giant know. Instead, Jack yelled out, "I can do something you can't do. I can squeeze water from a rock." The giant was astounded. He was so surprised at what Jack said that he did not eat Jack.

The two-headed giant said, "If you can do it, I can do it, too." Jack pretended to pick up a rock, but what he really did was pull big hunks of cheese from the enormous pouch under his jacket. He squeezed the cheese, and whey came out. Cheese is made from milk, and whey is the watery part of milk. The astounded giant tried to do the same. It squeezed rock after rock, but nothing came out. The giant was so upset that he ran away. He did not want anyone to know that a small boy was stronger than he was.

Jack and the Two-Headed Giant

After reading the story, answer the questions.
Fill in the circle next to the correct answer.

1. Where did the giant live?
   - ⓐ on land Jack needed to clear
   - ⓑ on land settled by the English
   - ⓒ in a land anthropologists studied
   - ⓓ in the mountains of North Carolina

2. This story is mainly about
   - ⓐ a boy named Jack
   - ⓑ storytelling customs
   - ⓒ what anthropologists study
   - ⓓ a story that has been passed down

3. When one is astounded, one is
   - ⓐ afraid
   - ⓑ terrible
   - ⓒ squeezed
   - ⓓ surprised

4. What might anthropologists learn about people from the story about Jack?
   - ⓐ They ate cheese.
   - ⓑ They got rid of giants.
   - ⓒ They wanted to be strong.
   - ⓓ They could squeeze water from rocks.

5. Think about how the word *small* relates to *enormous*. What words relate in the same way?

small : enormous

   - ⓐ tale : story
   - ⓑ cheese : whey
   - ⓒ horrible : nice
   - ⓓ anthropologist : scientist

A Game that Used Peach Baskets

These are new words to practice.

Say each word 10 times.

* instructor	* activity
* physical	* offense
* education	* curve
* required	* balcony

Before or after reading the story, write one sentence that contains at least one new word.

_____

_____

_____

A Game that Used Peach Baskets

In 1891, Dr. James Naismith wanted a game. Naismith was an instructor. He taught teachers how to be physical-education instructors. Naismith's teachers were required to go to class. When something is required, it is needed and has to be done. An hour of physical-education activity was also required.

In the fall, the teachers played football. In the spring, they played baseball. Football and baseball were played outside. They were good games for the teachers. The games provided a good hour of physical activity. But Naismith wanted another game. He wanted a game that could be played in the winter. He wanted a game that could be played indoors or in the evening.

Naismith decided he would make his own game. To make his game, Naismith thought about other games. All the team games he thought of had balls. Naismith's game would have a ball. Naismith thought about football. Football was rough. It was rough because the offense, the attacking team, could run with the ball. The offense is the team trying to make a goal. Naismith did not want a rough game. His game would not allow the offense to run with the ball like in football.

Naismith decided that in his game the ball could only be handled with one's hands. It could not be kicked. Naismith decided on a goal. He wanted a goal where the ball had to be thrown in a curve. If a ball had to be thrown in a curve, the ball could not be thrown with too much force.

Dr. James Naismith

What did Naismith use for his goal? Peach baskets! An old peach basket was nailed up at each end of the gym. The baskets were nailed to the gym's balcony railing. The peach baskets were nailed to the balcony railing at almost the exact height game hoops are placed today! Naismith's first ball was an old leather soccer ball. Today, Naismith's game is played all year 'round with its own special ball. It is played indoors and outdoors. It is played in the morning and evening. It is the game of basketball.

A Game that Used Peach Baskets

After reading the story, answer the questions.
Fill in the circle next to the correct answer.

1. When did Naismith's students play football?

   (a) in the fall

   (b) in the summer

   (c) in the winter

   (d) in the spring

2. Why did Naismith make it so a basketball had to curve to make a goal?

   (a) He did not want the players to kick the ball.

   (b) He did not want the players to run with the ball.

   (c) He did not wanted the players to have to play outdoors.

   (d) He did not want the players to throw the ball with too much force.

3. This story is mainly about

   (a) what led to a new game

   (b) how ballgames are made

   (c) when and how basketball is played today

   (d) how physical education teachers go to school

4. From the story, you can tell that Naismith most probably thought that

   (a) football was the roughest game

   (b) physical activity should go on all year

   (c) his new game was better than other games

   (d) all teachers should be physical-education instructors

5. Think about how the word *allow* relates to *let*. What words relate in the same way?

   allow : let

   (a) play : game

   (b) force : curve

   (c) require : need

   (d) instructor : physical

On Top of the World

These are new words to practice.

Say each word 10 times.

* floes

* brutal

* fortunately

* amputated

* attempt

* plunged

* toll

* accomplishment

Before or after reading the story, write one sentence
that contains at least one new word.

_____

_____

_____

On Top of the World

When standing at the North Pole, the only way one can go is south. That is where explorers Mathew Henson and Robert Peary wanted to be. They wanted to be first to the North Pole. To accomplish this, Henson and Peary would have to go where there was no land. They would have to travel on the frozen Arctic Ocean, crossing ice floes. They would have to climb towering hills of ice floes crushed together. They would have to be careful not to fall through cracks in the ice.

The two men had already tried twice before. The first time they almost starved to death. The men had walrus meat to eat, but the walrus meat was not fresh.

It was frozen solid, and the men could not eat it. When they tried to bite it, they cut the insides of their mouths. Fortunately, Henson was able to shoot a walrus. The men and their dogs feasted on the warm, bloody meat. Henson called that attempt "a long race with death."

On the men's second attempt, a terrible toll (price) was paid. The toll was due to the cruel, brutal cold. Peary's toes had frozen in the cruel, brutal cold. Eight toes had to be amputated, or cut off. Peary had trouble walking the rest of his life because of his amputated toes. Still, he and Henson would not give up their dream.

On their third and final attempt, Henson and Peary went with four Inuit. The Inuit were native people to the cold north. Disaster struck when Henson fell through the ice and plunged into the freezing Arctic Ocean. Fortunately, Ootah, one of the Inuit, saved him from his plunge by yanking Henson out by his hood.

On April 6, 1909, the two men accomplished what they set out to do. They stood at the North Pole. Henson was not given credit for their accomplishment for many years. This was because of the color of his skin. Henson was black; Peary was white. Today, both men are recognized for their accomplishment.

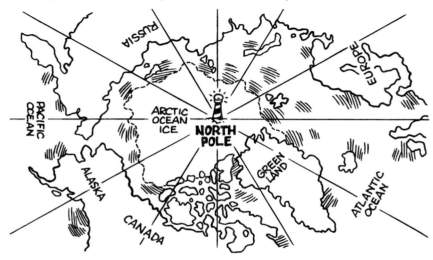

On Top of the World

**After reading the story, answer the questions.
Fill in the circle next to the correct answer.**

1. How many attempts did the two explorers make together for the North Pole?

   ⓐ 1

   ⓑ 2

   ⓒ 3

   ⓓ 4

2. Why did Peary have trouble walking?

   ⓐ He was starving.

   ⓑ He fell through the ice.

   ⓒ He had to have eight toes amputated.

   ⓓ He had to climb towering hills of ice.

3. This story is mainly about

   ⓐ reaching the North Pole

   ⓑ the frozen Arctic Ocean

   ⓒ a recognized accomplishment

   ⓓ a place where there is no land

4. What words best complete this sentence: "Each car has to pay _____ to cross the bridge."

   ⓐ a toll

   ⓑ a floe

   ⓒ a plunge

   ⓓ an attempt

5. Think about how the word *freezing* relates to *warm*. What words relate in the same way?

freezing : warm

   ⓐ floe : ice

   ⓑ brutal : nice

   ⓒ attempt : try

   ⓓ feasting : eat

How an Observation Helped Train a Horse

These are new words to practice.
Say each word 10 times.

✳ groom	✳ Macedonia
✳ attention	✳ tutor
✳ observation	✳ patience
✳ noticed	✳ determination

**Before or after reading the story, write one sentence
that contains at least one new word.**

_____

_____

_____

How an Observation Helped Train a Horse

The horse was wild. The king's grooms could not control it. None of the grooms could brush or clean it. None of the grooms could care for it or train it. They could not manage the horse at all. The king's son was only eight or nine years old. But the king's son paid attention. He made observations. He noticed what was going on about him. The king's son noticed something about the horse. Who was the king's son, and what observation did he make?

The king's son was born in 356 B.C. He was named Alexander. Alexander's father was king of Macedonia. At that time, Macedonia was a kingdom just north of Greece. When Alexander was young, he had a good tutor. The tutor's name was Aristotle. Aristotle was a great thinker. He taught Alexander a lot. Alexander paid attention to his tutor. He learned science. He learned geography. He read books.

Alexander watched the wild and unmanageable horse. He noticed that the horse acted wild because it was afraid of something. It was afraid of its own shadow! Alexander decided to train the horse. He was young, but he would do it alone. First, he talked gently to the horse. Then, he made it so the horse could not see its shadow. He did this by turning the horse to face the sun.

Alexander trained the horse with patience and determination. When one is patient, one works or waits steadily without complaining. When one is determined, one does not give up. What did Alexander's father say when he observed what his son had done? He told Alexander that he would have to find another kingdom. He told him that Macedonia wasn't going to be big enough for him.

Today we know Alexander as Alexander the Great. Alexander became king when his father was killed. He began to enlarge his kingdom by conquering surrounding countries. He made an empire. The empire extended across three continents. What horse did Alexander ride on his conquests? The same horse he had trained as a young boy!

How an Observation
Helped Train a Horse

After reading the story, answer the questions.
Fill in the circle next to the correct answer.

1. Macedonia was a kingdom just
   - (a) east of Greece
   - (b) west of Greece
   - (c) south of Greece
   - (d) north of Greece

2. From the story, you can tell that most probably Alexander
   - (a) was taught to ride by his tutor
   - (b) never rode horses that the grooms could manage
   - (c) observed the horse he trained at different times and days
   - (d) only conquered surrounding countries so that he could ride his horse

3. This story is mainly about
   - (a) Alexander
   - (b) an observation
   - (c) an empire long ago
   - (d) how to train a horse

4. Why do you think Alexander's father told Alexander he would have to find another kingdom?
   - (a) He did not want to share his kingdom.
   - (b) He wanted Alexander to enlarge his empire for him.
   - (c) He saw that Alexander didn't need to be taught by his tutor any longer.
   - (d) He knew Alexander's patience and determination would lead to greatness.

5. Think about how the word *hidden* relates to *observed*. What words relate in the same way?

hidden : observed

   - (a) wild : managed
   - (b) horse : groomed
   - (c) empire : conquered
   - (d) patient : determined

A Race for the Strong

These are new words to practice.

Say each word 10 times.

✳ marathon	✳ Persian
✳ endurance	✳ required
✳ physically	✳ Olympic
✳ grueling	✳ distance

Before or after reading the story, write one sentence that contains at least one new word.

_____

_____

_____

A Race for the Strong

A marathon is an endurance race. It is a race for the strong. Why is a marathon a race of endurance? Why is it a race for the strong? A marathon is a long foot race. It is 26 miles, 385 yards (42.2 km). To run this far, one must have great endurance. One must be physically strong. One must be able to hold up to great physical stress.

The history of this grueling race dates back to a battle. When something is grueling, it is very tiring. The battle took place during the Persian Wars. The battle was between the Persian Empire and the Greeks. It was in the year 490 B.C. The battle took place on a plain called Marathon.

The Greeks were greatly outnumbered, but they were highly trained. They charged into battle. After several hours, the Persians were defeated and fled the plain. The Greeks had won. After the battle, a man was chosen. The man was given a task. His task required endurance. What was his task? His task was to run. He was to run from Marathon to Athens. In Athens, he would tell people of the Persians' defeat. He would tell the people of Athens not to give up their city without a fight.

The man ran from Marathon to Athens. His long run was grueling. He ran it at top speed without stopping to rest. When he reached Athens, he relayed the news. He said, "Rejoice, we conquer!" Then, he died. In 1896, a marathon race was included in the first modern Olympic Games in Athens. The race was in honor of the long-ago runner. It was 26 miles (41.6 km). This was about the distance the man had been required to run to relay his news.

All marathons today are a little longer than the one in the first modern Olympic Games. Distance was added in 1908. Why? That year, the Olympic Games were in England. The King of England wanted the race to begin at Windsor Castle. Windsor Castle was 385 yards (352 meters) from the city's Olympic Stadium.

A Race for the Strong

After reading the story, answer the questions.
Fill in the circle next to the correct answer.

1. This story is mainly about
   - (a) how long a marathon is
   - (b) the modern Olympic Games
   - (c) an endurance race and its history
   - (d) a battle on the plain of Marathon

2. In what year was the first marathon included in the Olympics?
   - (a) 1826
   - (b) 1896
   - (c) 1908
   - (d) 1990

3. Why should marathons always be the same distance?
   - (a) so that runners around the world can get physically stronger
   - (b) so that runners around the world can run short marathons first
   - (c) so that runners around the world can start where kings can see them
   - (d) so that runners around the world can see who can run the same distance fastest

4. Think about how the word *battling* relates to *fighting*. What words relate in the same way?

battling : fighting

   - (a) running : racing
   - (b) grueling : tiring
   - (c) defeating : winning
   - (d) relaying : requiring

5. Which word best completes this sentence? "I am so hot," said Brett. "I don't know if I can _____ this heat much longer."
   - (a) relay
   - (b) battle
   - (c) endure
   - (d) conquer

Escape in the Open

These are new words to practice.

Say each word 10 times.

* Philadelphia   * bandage

* journey   * injuries

* accomplish   * separately

* accompany   * recognized

Before or after reading the story, write one sentence that contains at least one new word.

_____

_____

_____

Escape in the Open

Ellen Craft was a slave in Georgia. What Ellen hated most about slavery was that children could be taken from their parents. Ellen knew how much this hurt because she had been stolen away from her mother when she was a little girl. One night Ellen and her husband William decided to run away. They would run away to Philadelphia, a free city in Pennsylvania. This was a journey of 1,000 miles (1,609 kilometers). How could they accomplish their goal?

The Crafts made a daring plan to escape in the open. Ellen was very light-skinned. She would cut her hair and dress as a white man. A white man could make a journey alone with a male slave. A white woman could not. Ellen's husband would accompany her. He would go with her, traveling as her slave. Ellen would put on dark glasses. She would bandage her face. She would bandage her arm and put it in a sling.

If asked questions, Ellen could tell people that she was journeying to see a special doctor about her injuries. She could use her "injured" arm to explain why she could not sign papers. (At that time, it was against the law to teach slaves to read and write. People would know something was not right if they knew Ellen could not read or write.) The Crafts set off on the night of December 21, 1848. They walked to the train station separately. Ellen bought the tickets. Her husband could not accompany her to her seat. He had to ride in a separate car for slaves.

On the train, a man sat down next to Ellen. Ellen knew him! She was afraid she would be recognized. But the man never recognized Ellen. He never knew he was talking to a terrified runaway slave! In Savannah, Georgia, the Crafts boarded a boat. Ellen had to sleep in a room with white men. William had to sleep on the open deck. After one more train ride, the Crafts made it to Philadelphia. They had accomplished their goal by escaping in the open.

Escape in the Open

After reading the story, answer the questions.
Fill in the circle next to the correct answer.

1. This story is mainly about
   (a) slavery
   (b) a daring escape
   (c) going to Philadelphia
   (d) dressing as a white man

2. When did the Crafts begin their journey?
   (a) December 21, 1846
   (b) December 23, 1846
   (c) December 21, 1848
   (d) December 23, 1848

3. Why did Ellen need to put her arm in a sling?
   (a) so she could not be recognized
   (b) so she could be accompanied by her slave
   (c) so she could say she was going to see a doctor
   (d) so she could explain why she could not sign papers

4. Think about how the word *afraid* relates to *terrified*. What word relate in the same way?

afraid : terrified

   (a) escape : slavery
   (b) accomplish : goal
   (c) recognized : known
   (d) accompany : separate

5. Why did Ellen dress up like a man?
   (a) She was light-skinned.
   (b) Women did not wear dark glasses.
   (c) A woman would not go to a doctor.
   (d) Women could not travel alone with male slaves.

Record Temperatures

These are new words to practice.

Say each word 10 times.

* record	* Fahrenheit
* abrupt	* Celsius
* temperature	* discarded
* event	* average

Before or after reading the story, write one sentence
that contains at least one new word.

_____

_____

_____

Record Temperatures

On January 22, 1943, something happened. A record was made. The record was for the most abrupt temperature change in the United States. When something is abrupt, it happens suddenly. It comes without warning. The record event took place in Spearfish, South Dakota. The temperature was cold. The temperature was below freezing. It was -4° Fahrenheit (-20° Celsius). Then, it warmed up. It warmed up to 45° Fahrenheit (7° Celsius). The change was abrupt. The change happened in just two minutes!

Browning, Montana, holds a different record. It holds the record for the greatest range of temperatures over a 24-hour period. The record event took place January 23–24, 1916. The day's low was below freezing. It was -56° Fahrenheit (-49° Celsius). Then, it warmed up. The day's high was 44° Fahrenheit (7° Celsius).

Think about how we dress for the weather. Think about how the people in Spearfish and Browning dressed. They started out dressed for cold weather. They would have worn hats and mittens. They would have worn heavy coats and thick, long pants. Then, as it warmed up, they would have discarded their heavy clothing. When something is discarded, it is gotten rid of.

There is one place in the United States where it is easy to dress for the weather. The place is on top of Mount Wai´ale´ale. Mount Wai´ale´ale is in Hawaii. It is on the island of Kauai. How does one dress for Mount Wai´ale´ale? It is easy. One should always bring a raincoat. The top of Mount Wai´ale´ale is the wettest place in the United States. It rains an average of 460 inches (1,168 centimeters) a year!

Should one ever discard one's raincoat on Mount Wai´ale´ale? No, one's raincoat should never be discarded. This is because the top of Mount Wai´ale´ale is not just the wettest place in the United States. It is also the place where it has the greatest number of rainy days on average per year. How many days does it rain on average per year? 335 days!

Record Temperatures

After reading the story, answer the questions.
Fill in the circle next to the correct answer.

1. What place holds the record for the most abrupt temperature change?

   ⓐ Browning

   ⓑ Spearfish

   ⓒ United States

   ⓓ Mount Wai´ale´ale

2. This story is mainly about

   ⓐ rain in three places

   ⓑ changes in three places

   ⓒ weather in three places

   ⓓ temperature in three places

3. On average, how many days per year does it not rain on Mount Wai´ale´ale? (An average year has 365 days.)

   ⓐ 25

   ⓑ 30

   ⓒ 35

   ⓓ 40

4. Our game had _____ ending when it started to rain.

   ⓐ an abrupt

   ⓑ a discard

   ⓒ an average

   ⓓ a temperature

5. Think about how the word *heavy* relates to *light*. What words relate in the same way?

heavy : light

   ⓐ thick : thin

   ⓑ below : under

   ⓒ record : event

   ⓓ discard : remove

Buried Alive

These are new words to practice.

Say each word 10 times.

✻ sealing	✻ contained
✻ dome	✻ detected
✻ Paiute	✻ approaching
✻ constructed	✻ sage

**Before or after reading the story, write one sentence
that contains at least one new word.**

_____

_____

_____

Buried Alive

When Sarah Winnemucca was a little girl, she was buried alive. She was buried alongside her girl cousin. Winnemucca's mother and aunt felt they had no choice. It was the only way they knew to save the girls. Winnemucca's mother and aunt had been working hard sealing a large dome.

Sarah Winnemucca

Winnemucca was born in 1844. She was born in Nevada. She was a Native American, a member of the Northern Paiute tribe. The Northern Paiutes stored their winter food— dried fish and seeds—in specially-constructed domes. The domes were constructed from grass and mud. Then, they were sealed carefully so that the food they contained would remain safe until it was needed.

Just as Winnemucca's mother and aunt had finished sealing the dome, they detected people approaching. The people were not Paiutes. They were white. Winnemucca's mother and aunt grabbed their little girls and fled. They were afraid the approaching whites would kill and eat them. The little girls could not keep up. The mothers were determined to keep the girls safe. Determined to keep the girls alive, they buried them. Only the girls' faces were left uncovered.

The mother's covered the girls' faces with sage bushes. The sage bushes shielded the girls' faces from the hot sun. They told the girls to remain quiet and still. Then, the mothers ran and hid. All day, the girls had to lie without moving. All day, they had to lie without talking. All day, they had to worry that they would be found and eaten. The girls were not detected, but the white men found the dome. Then, the men did a terrible thing. They burned the dome and all of the food for winter it contained.

Winnemucca told this story to many people. She wanted to make sure that no other little girls ever had to be so fearful. To share her story, Winnemucca learned English. She spoke fearlessly in front of elegantly dressed crowds. She told about Paiute life. She told people that they needed to understand and treat her people better.

Buried Alive

After reading the story, answer the questions.
Fill in the circle next to the correct answer.

1. What was used to construct the domes?

    ⓐ fish

    ⓑ grass

    ⓒ seeds

    ⓓ sage bushes

2. Which answer lists what happened in the story in the right order?

    ⓐ the dome is sealed, the dome is built, the dome is burned

    ⓑ the girls run, the girls are covered with sage bush, the girls are buried

    ⓒ fish and seeds are collected, fish and seeds are stored, fish and seeds are dried

    ⓓ Winnemucca learns to speak English, Winnemucca speaks to crowds, Winnemucca speaks about her people

3. This story is mainly about

    ⓐ what the white men did

    ⓑ how Winnemucca wasn't detected

    ⓒ a Native American born in 1844

    ⓓ how Northern Paiutes stored their winter food

4. When something is seen or noticed, it is

    ⓐ sealed

    ⓑ detected

    ⓒ contained

    ⓓ constructed

5. Think about how the word *open* relates to *sealed*. What words relate in the same way?

open : sealed

    ⓐ quiet : still

    ⓑ shield : cover

    ⓒ construct : build

    ⓓ afraid : fearless

Valley Forge

These are new words to practice.

Say each word 10 times.

❊ decision   ❊ professionals

❊ suffered   ❊ amateurs

❊ defeat   ❊ harsh

❊ soldiers   ❊ lacked

Before or after reading the story, write one sentence that contains at least one new word.

_____

_____

_____

Valley Forge

General George Washington had to make a decision. His army had suffered a string of defeats. British soldiers were better trained. They were professionals. Washington's soldiers were amateurs. Amateurs are not professionals. The professional British Redcoats had badly beaten the American army so far. Would the American army be defeated completely? Would they lose the fight for independence?

Winter was coming on. It was 1777. The British troops had made themselves comfortable for the winter. They stayed in the city of Philadelphia. They stayed in warm houses. They stayed out of the snow and cold. Washington had to make a decision about his troops. Where would they stay for the harsh winter? Washington could move his troops to warm houses in cities far away. But then the British could advance.

Washington's decision was to keep the British from advancing. He chose to take his men to Valley Forge. Valley Forge was nothing but a high, rolling plain. It was just a few miles outside of Philadelphia.

The decision to stay at Valley Forge through the harsh winter was a hard one to make. It meant the British could not advance, but Washington's troops would suffer through the harsh winter.

Washington's men were ragged. They lacked clothing. They lacked proper clothes. They lacked boots. Many of the men had to wrap their feet in rags. Washington wrote, ". . . You might have tracked the army . . . to Valley Forge by the blood on their feet." The men had to build rough cabins. They had little food to eat while they worked. As the men worked, they chanted, "No bread, no meat, no bread, no meat!" One soldier on guard duty was seen standing on his hat to keep his bare feet out of the snow.

But Washington and his soldiers did not give up. They did not want to lose the fight for independence. They stayed in Valley Forge and suffered through the winter. In the spring, they trained hard. By the summer of 1778, the army was ready to fight. They were ready to show the British that they could not be defeated.

Valley Forge

**After reading the story, answer the questions.
Fill in the circle next to the correct answer.**

1. This story is mainly about
   ⓐ Washington's troops
   ⓑ General George Washington
   ⓒ the fight for independence
   ⓓ a decision to stay at Valley Forge

2. If you do not have something, you _____ it.
   ⓐ wrap
   ⓑ lack
   ⓒ chant
   ⓓ suffer

3. Think about how the word *amateur* relates to *professional*. What words relate in the same way?

amateur : professional

   ⓐ beat : defeat
   ⓑ fight : battle
   ⓒ make : decision
   ⓓ soldier : troops

4. Why was it a hard decision for Washington to take his men to Valley Forge?
   ⓐ It meant the British could advance.
   ⓑ It meant his men would have to stand guard duty.
   ⓒ It meant the British could stay in warm city houses.
   ⓓ It meant his men would suffer through the harsh winter.

5. From the story, you can tell that Washington's troops
   ⓐ were well fed
   ⓑ wanted independence
   ⓒ liked to suffer in the cold
   ⓓ did not like Washington's decision

Connecting Polygons to Month Names

These are new words to practice.
Say each word 10 times.

✻ polygon	✻ eleventh
✻ octagon	✻ twelfth
✻ nonagon	✻ festival
✻ decagon	✻ emperors

Before or after reading the story, write one sentence that contains at least one new word.

_____

_____

_____

Connecting Polygons to Month Names

What is a polygon? What could a polygon tell us about the names of months? A polygon is a closed, flat, figure. Polygons can have different numbers of sides, but every side is a straight line. A polygon with eight sides is called an octagon. A polygon with nine sides is called a nonagon. A polygon with ten sides is called a decagon.

Now think about the months October, November, and December. The names of those months start the same way *octagons, nonagons,* and *decagons* do. They start with *oct, no,* and *dec.* So why is October the tenth month, not the eighth month? Why is November the eleventh month, not the ninth month? Why is December the twelfth month, not the tenth month?

Our month names come from a calendar started by the Romans long ago. At first, the Roman calendar had only ten months, so October was the eighth month! November was the ninth month, and December was the tenth month. In Latin, the language of the Romans, *October* meant, "the eighth month. *November* meant "the ninth month." *December* meant "the tenth month."

When the Romans added the months January and February, the order of the months changed. October moved to tenth place. November moved to eleventh place. December moved to twelfth place. January was named after Janus, a Roman god with two faces. One face looked to the future. One face looked to the past. February was named after a Roman festival that happened at that time. The festival was called Februa. March, the first month in the first calendar, was named after Mars, the god of war.

The Romans named the month of April after the Latin word *aperire.* This word means "to open." May was named after Maia, the goddess of growth. June was named after the goddess of marriage or a powerful family with the last name of Junius. At first, July and August were called the fifth and sixth months in Latin. The names were changed to honor two emperors. The emperors were Julius Caesar and Augustus. In Latin, *September* meant "the seventh month," but today it is the ninth month.

That's an "octagon"!

Connecting Polygons
to Month Names

**After reading the story, answer the questions.
Fill in the circle next to the correct answer.**

1. What was the first month in the first Roman calendar named after?

   ⓐ Mars, the god of war

   ⓑ Februa, a Roman festival

   ⓒ Julius Caesar, an emperor

   ⓓ Maia, the goddess of growth

2. Using Latin, a decade most probably is

   ⓐ 9 years

   ⓑ 10 years

   ⓒ 11 years

   ⓓ 12 years

3. This story is mainly about

   ⓐ month names

   ⓑ people long ago

   ⓒ Roman gods and goddesses

   ⓓ polygons with different numbers of sides

4. The Romans most probably named the month of April after the Latin word *aperire* because at that time

   ⓐ many plants grew in Rome

   ⓑ many flower buds in Rome opened in that month

   ⓒ many marriages happened in Rome

   ⓓ many people looked forward to war

5. Think about how the word *clock* relates to *time*. What words relate in the same way?

clock : time

   ⓐ month : week

   ⓑ polygon : side

   ⓒ calendar : date

   ⓓ emperor : powerful

The Painter and His Horse

These are new words to practice.

Say each word 10 times.

✻ wilderness	✻ bulged
✻ passion	✻ unkempt
✻ observed	✻ tether
✻ species	✻ expensive

Before or after reading the story, write one sentence that contains at least one new word.

_____

_____

_____

The Painter and His Horse

John James Audubon is a famous painter. He was born in 1785. He traveled widely through the American wilderness. He developed a passion, or very strong feeling, for American birds. He observed them in the wilderness. He sketched them. He painted them. His passion was so great that he wanted something. He wanted to observe and paint every species, or kind, of American bird.

John James Audubon

Audubon went far and wide looking for every bird species. He had many adventures. For many of his travels, Audubon rode a horse named Barro. Audubon said that Barro was "not a handsome animal." He had a big head that bulged out. When something bulges, it swells out. Barro had a thin tail that dragged on the ground. Barro had a mane that was thick and unkempt. When something is unkempt, it is messy and uncombed.

Audubon bought Barro despite the way he looked. Audubon bought Barro from the Osage Native Americans. Audubon and Barro became very attached to each other. They were so attached that at night Audubon did not tether (tie up) Barro. Barro did not have to be tethered because he would not leave Audubon. In fact, Barro would not even drink until Audubon told him to. No matter how thirsty, Barro would wait for Audubon to give him the go ahead.

Once, Audubon came upon a man with an expensive horse. The man told Audubon all about his expensive horse. It cost hundreds of dollars. Then, the man said that he wished Audubon's horse were as good as his. Audubon didn't get upset. He just asked where the man hoped to get to that night. The man told Audubon he could join him for dinner at an inn if Audubon could get there.

Audubon said it was as if Barro understood. It was as if Barro knew that the man had said he was a cheap, bad horse. Barro just pricked up his ears. He went at a faster pace. What happened when the man showed up at the inn? Audubon was already there! He had already ordered dinner!

The Painter and His Horse

After reading the story, answer the questions.
Fill in the circle next to the correct answer.

1. This story is mainly about
   - ⓐ bird species
   - ⓑ painting birds
   - ⓒ Audubon and Barro
   - ⓓ adventures in the wilderness

2. What was not true about Barro?
   - ⓐ He had a big head.
   - ⓑ He was not handsome.
   - ⓒ He was attached to Audubon.
   - ⓓ He had a thick, unkempt tail.

3. Think about how the word *cheap* relates to *expensive*. What words relate in the same way?

cheap : expensive

   - ⓐ tether : tie
   - ⓑ observe : see
   - ⓒ unkempt : neat
   - ⓓ bulged : swelled

4. A proverb is an old, wise saying. Which proverb fits the story about Barro best?
   - ⓐ Every cloud has a silver lining.
   - ⓑ You can't judge a book by its cover.
   - ⓒ Don't put all your eggs in one basket.
   - ⓓ The bad workman always blames his tools.

5. Which word best fits in the blank: "Tom read day and night. Tom had a(n) _____ for reading."
   - ⓐ order
   - ⓑ passion
   - ⓒ adventure
   - ⓓ understanding

Where Water Glows in the Dark

These are new words to practice.

Say each word 10 times.

* favorite   * channel

* creatures   * Puerto Rico

* dinoflagellates   * citizen

* jostled   * spout

Before or after reading the story, write one sentence that contains at least one new word.

_____

_____

_____

Where Water Glows in the Dark

Juan has a favorite place. His favorite place is a special bay in his country. It is where water glows in the dark. The water glows because it is filled with billions of tiny creatures. In one gallon (3.8 liters) alone, there are 720,000 creatures! The tiny creatures are called dinoflagellates. The dinoflagellates produce a burst of light when they are jostled. When something is jostled, it is pushed or shoved in a rough way.

When Juan moves through the water, he leaves a glowing trail. This is because his movements jostle the billions of tiny creatures. Why are there so many dinoflagellates in the bay? The dinoflagellates are trapped. They cannot get out, as the bay is connected to the ocean with only one channel. The connecting channel is very narrow. Juan says, "They are like fireflies trapped in a bottle!"

Juan's special bay is part of Puerto Rico. Puerto Rico is an island. Puerto Rico is not a state. Still, it is part of the United States. How can this be? Long ago, Puerto Rico belonged to Spain. After the Spanish-American War in 1898, it became part of the United States. Juan is Puerto Rican. Still, he is a United States citizen. All Puerto Ricans were made citizens in 1917.

Juan likes to show visitors around the island. He takes them to see the glowing water. He also takes them to a rain forest. In the rain forest, Juan likes to show visitors special leaves. The leaves have little spouts. The leaves need the spouts to stay healthy. They need the spouts because of all the rain. Rain is channeled off of the leaves down the spouts. The spouts help keep the leaves from rotting and free of fungus.

Juan also likes to point out land creatures. His favorite is a tiny frog. The frog is only about an inch (2.5 centimeters) long. It is very noisy, and it lives in trees. There are 10,000 frogs per acre (.4 hectares) in the rain forest. Juan says, "What they don't have in size, they make up for in numbers!"

Where Water Glows in the Dark

**After reading the story, answer the questions.
Fill in the circle next to the correct answer.**

1. How many dinoflagellates are there per gallon (3.8 liters) of water?
   - ⓐ 720
   - ⓑ 7,200
   - ⓒ 72,000
   - ⓓ 720,000

2. What did Juan mean when he said, "What they don't have in size, they make up for in numbers!"
   - ⓐ Puerto Rican frogs are small and noisy.
   - ⓑ In Puerto Rico, people make up the numbers of frogs.
   - ⓒ There are lots of Puerto Rican frogs so they are small.
   - ⓓ Puerto Rican frogs may be small, but there are a lot of them!

3. This story is mainly about
   - ⓐ dinoflagellates in Puerto Rico
   - ⓑ what Juan likes in Puerto Rico
   - ⓒ where creatures live in Puerto Rico
   - ⓓ how Juan is a citizen in Puerto Rico

4. The story does not talk about
   - ⓐ how Puerto Ricans are citizens
   - ⓑ what people eat in Puerto Rico
   - ⓒ some creatures found in Puerto Rico
   - ⓓ when Puerto Rico became part of the United States

5. Think about how the word *trap* relates to *catch*. What words relate in the same way?

trap : catch

   - ⓐ jostle : shove
   - ⓑ channel : water
   - ⓒ number : billions
   - ⓓ dinoflagellate : glows

The Moon Festival

These are new words to practice.

Say each word 10 times.

* festival   * crescent

* celebrate   * waxing

* foreign   * waning

* invaders   * disappears

Before or after reading the story, write one sentence that contains at least one new word.

_____

_____

_____

China has many festivals. A festival is a happy holiday. It is a day or time of feasting or celebrating. One festival is the Moon Festival. The Moon Festival is celebrated around mid-September. It celebrates the season. Wheat and rice crops have been harvested. It is a happy time. It is a time to celebrate the harvest, get together, and eat mooncakes.

Mooncakes are round like the moon. They are good to eat. Long ago, in the 14th century, mooncakes were used to pass on secret messages. The secret messages were hidden in the mooncakes. The messages told when and where people should fight against foreign invaders. Foreign invaders are invaders that come from outside one's own country. Today, messages are still put on mooncakes. They are attached to the mooncake bottom or stuck on the box the cake came in.

People tell stories during the Moon Festival. One story goes like this: In a small village, two brothers each got a mooncake. Older Brother gulped his down in a hurry. Then, he said, "Younger Brother, would you like me to make your cake look more like the moon?" Younger Brother was very excited. He handed his cake to Older Brother. Older Brother quickly took a bite out of the cake. His bite made the round mooncake look like a crescent moon.

Younger Brother began to cry. Older Brother said, "You do not like your crescent moon? Here, let me give you a half moon." Then Older Brother ate more of the cake, biting off the ends of the crescent. Younger Brother was very upset. Older Brother calmed him down by describing all the moon phases. He described the waxing half moon. "The waxing half moon grows into a full moon," he said.

"After the full moon, there is a waning half moon," he said. "The waning moon gets smaller. This is when it disappears. It disappears and can't be seen anymore—just like your mooncake." Then Older Brother quickly gulped down the rest of Younger Brother's mooncake and skipped away!

The Moon Festival

**After reading the story, answer the questions.
Fill in the circle next to the correct answer.**

1. In what century were messages about when and where to fight foreign invaders hidden in mooncakes?

   (a) the 14th

   (b) the 16th

   (c) the 18th

   (d) the 20th

2. What is not true about the Moon Festival?

   (a) It is a time to tell stories.

   (b) It is a time to get together.

   (c) It is a time to celebrate the season.

   (d) It is a time to harvest wheat and rice.

3. This story is mainly about

   (a) two brothers

   (b) the moon festival

   (c) attached messages

   (d) celebrations in China

4. When the moon is waning, it is

   (a) a new moon

   (b) a full moon

   (c) getting bigger

   (d) getting smaller

5. Think about how the word *older* relates to *younger*. What words relate in the same way?

older : younger

   (a) secret : message

   (b) disappear : gone

   (c) slowly : quickly

   (d) round : crescent

A Race of Life and Death

These are new words to practice.

Say each word 10 times.

* medicine	* contagious
* certain	* relay
* diphtheria	* blizzard
* disease	* Siberian husky

Before or after reading the story, write one sentence that contains at least one new word.

_____

_____

_____

A Race of Life and Death

Medicine was needed. Children faced certain death. Diphtheria had spread around Nome, Alaska. Diphtheria is a disease. It is highly contagious. When something is contagious, it is spread by contact. It can be caught from someone else. Diphtheria causes high fevers. It causes sore throats. Without medicine, the disease often causes death.

Today children are protected from diphtheria. They are vaccinated when they are small. But this true story is not about today. This story happened in 1925. It was winter. The closest medicine was over 1,000 miles (1,609 kilometers) away. How could the medicine get to Nome? Who or what could make its way through the snow and ice?

The medicine could not come by train. In 1925, the nearest train line ended 675 miles (1,086 kilometers) away. The medicine could not come by plane. There were only two planes in Alaska at that time. Both planes had open cockpits. They were in storage for the winter. Only dogs could make the trip. Only dogs could get the medicine to the children.

A single driver and his sled-dog team could make the trip. But that would take about 20 days. In 20 days, many children would die. Instead, drivers set up a relay. Each team ran a distance. They ran day and night. They did not stop to eat. They did not stop to rest. They did not stop for blizzards. The dog that led the last relay distance was named Balto. Balto was a Siberian husky. Balto led his team of fellow Siberian huskies over 53 miles (85 kilometers).

Gunnar Kasson, Balto's driver, described the blizzard conditions. The temperature was 40 degrees below zero. The winds flipped the sled off the trail. Kasson was blinded by the snow. He could not see his hand in front of his face. He was not certain where he was. He had to depend completely on Balto. Balto led the team to Nome after pulling for 20 hours. Balto and the other dogs were so tired that they could not even bark. But the children were saved. The medicine arrived in just five-and-a-half days.

A Race of Life and Death

After reading the story, answer the questions.
Fill in the circle next to the correct answer.

1. This story is mainly about
   (a) a relay to bring medicine
   (b) winter blizzards in Alaska
   (c) a Siberian husky named Balto
   (d) how to save children from disease

2. Why did Gunnar Kasson have to depend on Balto?
   (a) Balto was a dog.
   (b) Kasson did not know where he was.
   (c) The blizzard winds had flipped the sled.
   (d) Kasson was tired from pulling for 20 hours.

3. Think about how the word *Siberian husky* relates to *dog*. What words relate in the same way?

   | **Siberian husky : dog** |

   (a) sled : driver
   (b) blizzard : snow
   (c) relay : distance
   (d) diphtheria : disease

4. Which word best fits in the blank? "When Emily laughed, we all laughed. Emily's laugh was _____ _____."
   (a) certain
   (b) medicine
   (c) a disease
   (d) contagious

5. By setting up a relay, how much faster did the men get the medicine to the children?
   (a) about 5 days faster
   (b) about 10 days faster
   (c) about 15 days faster
   (d) about 20 days faster

How Some Nicknames Came About

These are new words to practice.

Say each word 10 times.

* exercise

* equality

* nickname

* constitution

* badger

* tar

* residents

* retreated

Before or after reading the story, write one sentence that contains at least one new word.

_____

_____

_____

How Some Nicknames Came About

Ms. Rice said, "Class, I have a fun exercise for you. Each state has a nickname. I am going to say the nickname of a state. Let's see if you can match the state to the nickname. Let's see how well you can do on this exercise."

Ms. Rice's first question was about the Badger State. Ms. Rice wanted to know what state was nicknamed the Badger State. She wanted to know why the residents, or people who lived there, were known as Badgers. Dana knew the answer. She said, "Wisconsin is nicknamed the Badger State. Long ago, back in the early 1800s, miners mined lead in Wisconsin. Often, the miners lived in hillside caves they had dug. The caves the miners lived in reminded people of the way badgers dig holes. So the people called the miners badgers. Over time, all the residents of Wisconsin were called Badgers."

Ms. Rice's second question was about the Equality State. She wanted to know what state was nicknamed the Equality State and why. Brad knew the answer. He said, "Wyoming is the Equality State. Its nickname came about when it was still a territory. Wyoming's territorial constitution was the first to do something. It was the first constitution in the world to give women full voting rights. This was back in 1889. Wyoming became a state one year later, in 1890."

Next, Ms. Rice asked about the Tar Heel State. She wanted to know why the residents of this state were nicknamed Tar Heels. Kim knew the answer. He said, "The state is North Carolina. North Carolina produced tar. Tar was one of its first products. The nickname came from what some people said they would do with tar.

"The story goes that during a Civil War battle, the people from North Carolina had to fight alone. They had to fight alone because other members of the Confederate forces retreated. So the people of North Carolina said they would put tar on the heels of those who had retreated. That way they would 'stick better in the next fight.'"

How Some Nicknames Came About

After reading the story, answer the questions.
Fill in the circle next to the correct answer.

1. This story is mainly about
   - (a) exercise
   - (b) three state nicknames
   - (c) what some residents are called
   - (d) the children in Ms. Rice's class

2. Which student answered the question about the Badger State?
   - (a) Kim
   - (b) Dana
   - (c) Brad
   - (d) Rick

3. Which word best fills in the blank? "Ms. Rice's class had a pet goldfish. The goldfish was a classroom _____."
   - (a) product
   - (b) exercise
   - (c) resident
   - (d) constitution

4. Think about how the word *back* relates to *forward*. What words relate in the same way?

   back : forward

   - (a) badger : hole
   - (b) battle : fight
   - (c) nickname : state
   - (d) retreat : advance

5. From the story, you can tell that
   - (a) some states do not have nicknames
   - (b) tar is no longer produced in North Carolina
   - (c) women have not always had the right to vote
   - (d) Wisconsin is the only state where lead is mined

The Toilet-Paper Trail

These are new words to practice.

Say each word 10 times.

* Everest   * oxygen

* unfortunately   * toilet

* supplies   * hired

* equipment   * deposit

Before or after reading the story, write one sentence that contains at least one new word.

_____

_____

_____

The Toilet-Paper Trail

Mount Everest is a mountain. It is the highest mountain in the world. It is 29,035 feet (8,850 meters) high. This is higher above sea level than anywhere else on Earth. Many people want to climb mountains. Many mountain climbers want to climb Everest. People have been asked why they want to climb mountains. George Mallory, a climber who died on Everest, is said to have answered, "Because it's there."

Unfortunately, there is also trash. Many people travel to Everest every year. They bring tons of supplies. They bring the things they need. They bring food. They bring stoves and fuel in bottles for the stoves. They bring climbing equipment, like ropes and tents. Many climbers bring bottles of oxygen. They breathe the oxygen as they climb. They do this because the air is very thin high on Everest. A few people have climbed Everest without bottled oxygen. But most climbers use bottled oxygen. They would not make it to the top without it.

All the people and supplies mean a lot of trash. There are not any trashcans. There are not any toilets. So people leave their trash everywhere. Broken equipment is left. Empty oxygen bottles are left. Human waste is left. Trash has been left for over 50 years. The trash has begun to pile up. So much waste has been left that the trail up Everest has been called the Toilet-Paper Trail.

The problem is that climbers hired people to carry supplies in. Unfortunately, they did not hire people to carry supplies out. All they cared about was climbing the mountain. Fortunately, some people are trying to clean up Everest. They do not want Everest to be the highest trash dump. They do not want the trail up Everest to be the Toilet-Paper Trail.

Ways are being found to clean up the mountain. Today, for example, the government of Nepal makes climbers pay a deposit. The climbers must pay the government several thousand dollars. The climbers can get their deposit back. They get it back only if they take out their trash and human waste.

The Toilet-Paper Trail

After reading the story, answer the questions.
Fill in the circle next to the correct answer.

1. This story is mainly about
   a) trash on Everest
   b) toilet paper on Everest
   c) mountain climbers on Everest
   d) carrying supplies on Everest

2. What is unfortunate about the climbers on Everest?
   a) The climbers bring tons of supplies.
   b) The climbers leave their human waste.
   c) The climbers want to climb the mountain.
   d) The climbers use bottled oxygen in the thin air.

3. When someone is hired,
   a) one puts down a deposit
   b) one uses bottled oxygen
   c) one is paid to do a job
   d) one is a mountain climber

4. Think about how the word *trail* relates to *road*. What words relate in the same way?

trail : road

   a) deposit : pay
   b) trash : carry
   c) hill : mountain
   d) equipment : tent

5. From the story, you can tell that
   a) trashcans will be put on Everest
   b) supplies will no longer be carried up Everest
   c) people will stop using bottled oxygen on Everest
   d) there is not much oxygen on top of Everest

What Stanton Dreaded

These are new words to practice.

Say each word 10 times.

* belonged   * drawn

* equal   * dreaded

* audiences   * swarms

* complained   * received

Before or after reading the story, write one sentence that contains at least one new word.

_____

_____

_____

What Stanton Dreaded

Elizabeth Cady Stanton was born in 1815. She was born in Johnstown, New York. When Stanton was born, women were not allowed to vote. Women had very few rights. If a woman married, she became her husband's property. All that she owned belonged to her husband. All that she earned belonged to her husband. It was her husband who could choose what to do with their children. This was the law.

Stanton worked hard for equal rights. She wanted women to count just as much as men. She wanted women and men to be equal under the law. She wanted all citizens to have the right to vote. In 1867, Stanton spoke all over Kansas about the importance of equal rights. She spoke to audiences in log cabins, schools, and churches. She spoke to audiences in hotels, barns, and even the open air.

Elizabeth Cady Stanton

The white-haired, plump, merry grandmother never complained as she made her way from crowd to crowd in a mule-drawn carriage. She never complained, but there was one thing she dreaded, or feared. What did Stanton dread?

Stanton often traveled in her mule-drawn carriage far into the night. When she would come across a log cabin, she would ask for shelter. The people were always welcoming, offering Stanton a bed while its owners slept on the floor. Then, all night, Stanton would be bitten! She would be bitten by swarms of bedbugs. Stanton even tried sleeping with her clothes on, but nothing kept the swarms of bedbugs from biting her.

One time, Stanton felt something run across her head. She thought it might be a mouse. In the morning, Stanton mentioned the possible mouse. The owner simply said that they thought there was a mouse nest in the bed, as they had heard lots of squeaking in the past week! Despite the dreadful sleeping conditions, Stanton enjoyed traveling across Kansas. Stanton died before women received the right to vote, but her work helped make it all possible. Stanton died in 1902. Women received the right to vote in 1920.

What Stanton Dreaded

After reading the story, answer the questions.
Fill in the circle next to the correct answer.

1. When Stanton married her husband,
   - (a) she could vote
   - (b) she had very few rights
   - (c) she had to earn her own money
   - (d) she was equal with her husband under the law

2. This story is mainly about
   - (a) bedbugs
   - (b) equal rights
   - (c) Stanton's work
   - (d) the right to vote

3. How many years after Stanton died did women receive the right to vote?
   - (a) 16
   - (b) 18
   - (c) 20
   - (d) 22

4. From the story, one can tell that Stanton was known as being
   - (a) sad
   - (b) poor
   - (c) selfish
   - (d) cheerful

5. Think about how the word *dreaded* relates to *feared*. What words relate in the same way?

dreaded : feared

   - (a) pulled : drawn
   - (b) swarm : bedbugs
   - (c) received : belonged
   - (d) complained : enjoyed

The Geographic Center

These are new words to practice.

Say each word 10 times.

* geographic   * frontier

* extends   * region

* produces   * aloha

* ranks   * archipelago

**Before or after reading the story, write one sentence
that contains at least one new word.**

_____

_____

_____

The Geographic Center

The United States has a geographic center. The geographic center is the middle. It is the middle of the United States. From the center, the United States extends the same distance east as west. It extends the same distance north as south. The geographic center moved in 1959. Before, it was in Lebanon, Kansas.

Kansas's nickname is the Sunflower State. Sunflowers grow in Kansas, but so does wheat. Kansas produces a lot of wheat. It produces so much wheat that it is sometimes known as our nation's breadbasket. Kansas became a state in 1861. It was the 34th state. It ranks 13th in size. So why did the geographic center change in 1959? Why was it no longer in Kansas? Where is it today?

In 1959, two new states joined the union. One of the states was Alaska. Alaska's nickname is the Last Frontier. The frontier is the part of a settled country that lies next to a region that it still unsettled. It lies next to a region that is still a wilderness. Even today, large parts of Alaska are wild and unsettled. Alaska was the 49th state. It ranks 1st in size. It totals one-sixth of the country's entire area!

The 50th state to join the union was Hawaii. It was the last state to join. Hawaii's nickname is the Aloha State. "Aloha" is a native Hawaiian word. It is a greeting. It means both "hello" and "goodbye." Hawaii is an archipelago. An archipelago is a chain of closely grouped islands. Hawaii has eight main islands. It has 132 islands in total. It ranks 47th in size. The new states made the United States bigger. The new land made a new middle.

The geographic center moved. It moved from Kansas. It moved to a point near Belle Fourche, South Dakota. South Dakota's nickname is the Mount Rushmore State. The faces of four presidents are carved into Mount Rushmore. One face is George Washington's. One face is Thomas Jefferson's. One face is Theodore Roosevelt's. One face is Abraham Lincoln's. South Dakota became a state in 1889. It was the 40th state. It ranks 16th in size.

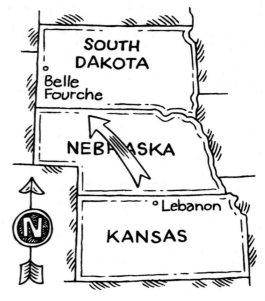

The Geographic Center

After reading the story, answer the questions.
Fill in the circle next to the correct answer.

1. This story is mainly about
   - (a) the geographic center of the United States and state size
   - (b) where the geographic center of the United States is today
   - (c) state nicknames and the geographic center of the United States
   - (d) why the United States geographic center is where it is and state information

2. Which answer correctly lists the states from smallest to biggest in size?
   - (a) Alaska, South Dakota, Kansas, Hawaii
   - (b) Hawaii, Kansas, South Dakota, Alaska
   - (c) Hawaii, South Dakota, Kansas, Alaska
   - (d) Kansas, Hawaii, Alaska, South Dakota

3. Think about how the word *archipelago* relates to *island*. What words relate in the same way?

archipelago : island

   - (a) herd : cow
   - (b) puppy : dog
   - (c) cat : kitten
   - (d) chicken : flock

4. Which state has a mountain with four presidents carved into it?
   - (a) Hawaii
   - (b) Kansas
   - (c) Alaska
   - (d) South Dakota

5. From the story, you can tell that the geographic center of the United States
   - (a) will never change again
   - (b) was always in Kansas until 1959
   - (c) changes when new states are added
   - (d) is closer to the north than the south

A Key to Mongol Horsemanship

These are new words to practice.

Say each word 10 times.

* Mongols	* Genghis Khan
* Eurasian	* organized
* steppe	* brigades
* vast	* stirrup

Before or after reading the story, write one sentence that contains at least one new word.

_____

_____

_____

A Key to Mongol Horsemanship

The Mongols were a nomadic people. They did not stay in one place. They herded animals on the Eurasian steppe. The Eurasian steppe is a vast belt of dry grassland. It is an enormous wind-swept plain. One Mongol clan leader united the Mongols. This Mongol clan leader became known as Genghis Khan. Genghis Khan was born about 1162. He died in 1227.

Genghis Khan built a vast empire. He conquered much of Central Asia. He was very organized. He grouped his warriors. He organized them into armies. Each army had 10,000 warriors. The 10,000 warriors were organized into 1,000-man brigades. The brigades were organized into 100-man companies. The companies were organized into groups of ten.

When each army moved, it was like a moving city. Why? The Mongol families followed the army. No one was left behind. All the Mongol horses and livestock followed the army, too. Horses and livestock numbered in the tens of thousands.

The Mongols were superb horsemen. They were expert horsemen. They spent most of their lives in the saddle. Each warrior had three extra horses. By changing horses, a warrior did not have to stop. He could go far. He could go 120 miles (193 kilometers) per day. He could stay in the saddle a long time. He could remain on a horse for ten days and nights at a time! Sometimes, Mongols used their horses to keep from starving. They would make a small gash in a horse's neck. Then, they would drink the horse's blood.

There was a key to Mongol horsemanship. The key was invented in the second century B.C. It was invented on the steppe. It let the warrior do something while on his horse. What did it let him do? It let him stand, turn, and shoot arrows behind him. What let the warrior do this? What was invented? What was the key?

It was the stirrup! A warrior could stand in his stirrups. Then, he could turn and shoot arrows behind him.

A Key to Mongol Horsemanship

After reading the story, answer the questions.
Fill in the circle next to the correct answer.

1. This story is mainly about
   - (a) a key
   - (b) organized armies
   - (c) the Eurasian steppe
   - (d) expert horsemen of long ago

2. How many warriors were in a Mongol brigade?
   - (a) 10
   - (b) 100
   - (c) 1,000
   - (d) 10,000

3. Think about how the word *gash* relates to *cut*. What words relate in the same way?

gash : cut

   - (a) go : remain
   - (b) foot : stirrup
   - (c) vast : enormous
   - (d) leader : conquered

4. What would one not expect to find on a steppe?
   - (a) trees
   - (b) grass
   - (c) plains
   - (d) animals

5. Why didn't Genghis Khan have to worry about his warriors leaving to take care of their families?
   - (a) Families followed the armies.
   - (b) The warriors had three extra horses.
   - (c) Genghis Khan had united the Mongols.
   - (d) The nomadic people did not stay in one place.

History Humor

These are new words to practice.

Say each word 10 times.

* seriously	* quiver
* title	* judges
* humor	* supreme
* geologist	* court

**Before or after reading the story, write one sentence
that contains at least one new word.**

_____

_____

_____

History Humor

"Class," Ms. Deer said seriously, "you are not working hard enough. I am going to hand you a booklist. You will find a title you like on the list and read the book." The students in Ms. Deer's class groaned. They did not mind working, but today was supposed to be a special day. Ms. Deer had told them that today was going to be "History Humor Day."

Humor is the quality of being funny. The students thought that "History Humor Day" would be fun. They thought they would be learning about funny times in history. Then the students looked at the booklist Ms. Deer was handing out. They started to laugh at the book titles. They realized that Ms. Deer was not being serious. She had played a humorous trick on them.

Grinning, Eric said, "I enjoy planes. I enjoy learning about the first people who flew a plane. I will read *The Wright Brothers* by Juan Toofly." Sandy liked reading about the presidents, so she said she would read *George Washington Runs for President* by Betty Winz. Mahendra liked geography, so he said he would read *The Grand Canyon* by Watt A. Landmark.

Dave wanted to be a geologist one day. He wanted to study the times the Earth's crust trembles, shakes, and quivers. He said he would read the book *The San Francisco Earthquake* by I. Quiver. Shina, quivering with laughter, said, "I don't want to be a geologist, but I do want to be one of the nine judges on the Supreme Court. The Supreme Court is the highest court in the land. I will read *Nine Judges* by Sue Preemcourt."

Lillian said she would read *The Pilgrims' Voyage to America* by May Flower. She said she might learn the name of the ship the Pilgrims sailed on if she read that book. Jack said he would read *The Adventures of Lewis and Clark* by X. Plorwest to find out what Lewis and Clark did. Ms. Deer laughed at what Lillian and Jack said. She was glad everyone was enjoying the pretend book titles.

History Humor

After reading the story, answer the questions.
Fill in the circle next to the correct answer.

1. This story is mainly about
   (a) real books
   (b) funny books
   (c) pretend books
   (d) humorous books

2. What would most likely quiver in the wind?
   (a) cars
   (b) rocks
   (c) houses
   (d) leaves

3. Think about how the word *pretend* relates to *real*. What words relate in the same way?

pretend : real

   (a) sail : boat
   (b) serious : humorous
   (c) grinning : laughing
   (d) geography : geologist

4. What did Lewis and Clark most probably do?
   (a) explore the West
   (b) explore the East
   (c) explore the South
   (d) explore the North

5. When did the children in Ms. Deer's class groan?
   (a) after they read the book titles
   (b) before they knew Ms. Deer was not serious
   (c) after they picked the books they were going to read
   (d) before Ms. Deer told them it was "History Humor Day"

"I Have Not Yet Begun to Fight"

These are new words to practice.

Say each word 10 times.

* naval   * Continental

* escorting   * sloshed

* convoy   * gaping

* merchant   * surrender

Before or after reading the story, write one sentence that contains at least one new word.

_____

_____

_____

"I Have Not Yet Begun to Fight!"

John Paul Jones is a great American naval hero. Jones is perhaps best known for his battle with the *Serapis*. The *Serapis* was a large English warship. The *Serapis* was escorting, or sailing along with, a convoy of 42 merchant ships. The job of the *Serapis* was to protect the merchant ships in the convoy.

John Paul Jones

While at sea, Jones came upon the *Serapis*. It was September 23, 1779. This was a time of war. The American colonies were fighting the English. The colonies were fighting for independence. Jones was a naval commander for the Continental Navy. The Continental Navy was the navy of the American colonies during the Revolutionary War.

Jones wanted to capture the convoy. To capture the convoy, he would have to sink its escort, the *Serapis*. Jones led a small fleet. He thought that if his fleet shot together, they could sink the *Serapis*. Jones gave the order to fire. But none of the other ships in his fleet obeyed the order! Jones and his crew were left all alone. They were left alone in the ship the *Richard*.

Jones did not back down. His crew sloshed the decks with water. They sloshed water on the decks to keep them from catching on fire. Sharpshooters climbed into the riggings. Gunners went to their battle stations. At first, Jones' crew was beaten back. The guns of the *Serapis* pounded the *Richard*. The *Richard* had large, gaping holes in its sides. The *Richard* was badly damaged. Then, the two ships crashed into each other. The captain of the *Serapis* expected Jones to surrender.

Jones did not surrender. From his badly damaged ship, he yelled out, "I have not yet begun to fight!" The battle went on for two days. At one point, the two ships came together so tightly that the cannons from each ship were touching each other! Fires on the *Richard* were burning out of control. Water poured in through the gaping holes, and the ship was sinking. Still, Jones would not surrender. Finally, the *Serapis* surrendered. The *Richard* was beyond saving, but Jones had won the battle.

"I Have Not Yet Begun to Fight!"

After reading the story, answer the questions.
Fill in the circle next to the correct answer.

1. In the story, what war did Jones fight in?
   - (a) the English War
   - (b) the Colonies War
   - (c) the Revolutionary War
   - (d) the Continental Navy War

2. This story is mainly about
   - (a) a naval battle
   - (b) the American colonies
   - (c) the Revolutionary War
   - (d) what ship surrendered

3. Which word best fills in the blank? "Sarah's mouth _____ in surprise at the sight of the monkey on the teacher's desk."
   - (a) gaped
   - (b) sloshed
   - (c) escorted
   - (d) surrendered

4. When did Jones yell out, "I have not yet begun to fight"?
   - (a) before the battle
   - (b) after the *Serapis* surrendered
   - (c) after the *Richard* was damaged
   - (d) before the two boats crashed into each other

5. Think about how the word *large* relates to *small*. What words relate in the same way?

large : small

   - (a) sink : water
   - (b) fleet : ship
   - (c) fight : battle
   - (d) together : alone

John and Jane Doe

These are new words to practice.

Say each word 10 times.

* wandering   * tradition

* description   * lawyers

* broadcast   * fictitious

* unidentified   * represent

Before or after reading the story, write one sentence that contains at least one new word.

_____

_____

_____

John and Jane Doe

A man is found wandering. The man does not know who he is. A woman is found wandering. The woman does not know who she is. The police put out a description. The description includes eye, hair, and skin color. The description includes what the two were wearing. In the police reports, the man is called John Doe. The woman is called Jane Doe.

News broadcasts are made. The news is broadcast on the radio. It is broadcast on television. The broadcasts describe John and Jane Doe. People are asked to come forward with any information about the wandering couple. Why is the man given the name John Doe? Why is the woman called Jane Doe? All unidentified people are called John and Jane Doe. The police call people who cannot be identified John or Jane Doe. Hospitals, too, call all unidentified patients John or Jane Doe. When did this tradition start?

The roots of this tradition go back long ago. It began with lawyers. In early Roman times, lawyers used fictitious, or made up, names. They used the fictitious names when they tried cases. The fictitious names were supposed to represent the average or common man. Male names were Titus or Gaius. Female names were Sempronia or Cornelia. Bringing up the fictitious name helped a lawyer show what the case meant to the average man.

Centuries later, lawyers used a different fictitious name to show what a case meant to the average man. The lawyers were in Britain. The British lawyers used the most common name in England. They used the name John.

As time went on, a second name was added. For better identification, John was called John-a-land or John-a-farm. Then, in the 1300s, John Doe began to be used. Today, John Doe is used to represent the average man. Jane Doe is used to represent the average woman. John Doe and Jane Doe are also used for real people who cannot be identified.

John and Jane Doe

After reading the story, answer the questions.
Fill in the circle next to the correct answer.

1. What name was not used by lawyers to represent the common man?

   (a) John

   (b) Titus

   (c) Cornelia

   (d) Stephanie

2. This story is mainly about

   (a) the average man

   (b) a name tradition

   (c) names lawyers used

   (d) a wandering man and woman

3. From the story, you can tell that

   (a) lawyers do not represent the common man.

   (b) no real person has the name John or Jane Doe.

   (c) all wandering people cannot be identified.

   (d) John was a common name in Britain long ago.

4. Which word best fits in the blank? "Every year my grandmother tells the same story on my birthday. It is a family _____."

   (a) lawyer

   (b) broadcast

   (c) tradition

   (d) description

5. Think about how the word *unidentified* relates to *known*. What words relate in the same way?

unidentified : known

   (a) average : common

   (b) fictitious : real

   (c) information : news

   (d) description : color

A Boy with Cold Ears

These are new words to practice.

Say each word 10 times.

* shield	* champion
* muffler	* protector
* fiercely	* patent
* device	* manufacturer

Before or after reading the story, write one sentence that contains at least one new word.

_____

_____

_____

A Boy with Cold Ears

It was a winter day in 1873. Chester Greenwood walked to a pond that had frozen over. Greenwood wanted to try out a new pair of ice skates. Greenwood was a 15-year-old farm boy who lived in Maine. Greenwood wanted to skate, but he couldn't. His ears were too cold! His ears were so cold that they hurt.

Greenwood want home determined to find something to shield his ears. Many of Greenwood's friends wrapped their wool mufflers around their heads. A muffler is a scarf worn around the throat for warmth. Wrapping his muffler around his head was out of the question for Greenwood. This was because just the touch of wool made Greenwood's ears itch fiercely.

It didn't take Greenwood long to come up with a device. A device is something made or invented for some special use. Greenwood called his device the Greenwood Champion Ear Protector. The device was simple, but it kept one's ears warm even in fierce cold. The device consisted of a headband made out of soft wire. A flap was attached to each end of the headband. The flaps covered one's ears and shielded them from the cold. The flaps had beaver fur on the outside. On the inside part that touched the ear, the flaps had black velvet.

Greenwood had invented earmuffs! Greenwood's ear protectors were so popular that all of his friends wanted some, too. Greenwood was pleased that his invention was popular, but he was determined to make it better. He thought the flaps flapped too much. Greenwood changed materials. His new earmuffs had a springy steel headband. They also had a tiny hinge on each flap so that they would fit snugly against the ear.

Greenwood took out a patent on his invention when he was only 18 years old. A patent is a right given by the government. Greenwood's patent gave him the right to be the only manufacturer, or maker, of earmuffs for a certain number of years. Greenwood started up a factory to manufacture his earmuffs. Earmuffs were sold in the thousands. Even today, earmuffs remain champion sellers.

A Boy with Cold Ears

**After reading the story, answer the questions.
Fill in the circle next to the correct answer.**

1. This story is mainly about
   - (a) Greenwood's life
   - (b) a boy and an invention
   - (c) how to keep one's ears warm
   - (d) earmuffs and how they are made

2. What material was Greenwood's first headband made out of?
   - (a) soft wire
   - (b) beaver fur
   - (c) black velvet
   - (d) springy steel

3. Which of the following items could be a device?
   - (a) an apple
   - (b) an apple pie
   - (c) an apple tree
   - (d) an apple peeler

4. Think about how the word *muffler* relates to *throat*. What words relate in the same way?

muffler : throat

   - (a) hat : head
   - (b) bike : ride
   - (c) scarf : wool
   - (d) shirt : button

5. Why did Greenwood take out a patent on his invention?
   - (a) He wanted to start up a factory.
   - (b) He wanted to be the champion seller.
   - (c) He wanted to be the only person to manufacture it.
   - (d) He wanted to stop the flaps from flapping too much.

Why Wagons Were Called Ships

These are new words to practice.

Say each word 10 times.

* schooner   * Great Plains

* pioneers   * distance

* canvas   * oxen

* prairie   * passengers

Before or after reading the story, write one sentence that contains at least one new word.

_____

_____

_____

Why Wagons Were Called Ships

A schooner is a ship. It is a ship with two or three masts and sails that are set lengthwise. When pioneers traveled west, they often traveled in wagons. The wagons were made of wood. They were about the size of a minivan. Pioneers covered their wagons with white canvas, a strong, heavy cloth. The cloth was stretched over five or six U-shaped bows. These wagons were often called prairie schooners. How did a wagon get a ship's name?

As the pioneers traveled west, they had to cross the Great Plains. Much of the Great Plains was prairie. A prairie is a large area of flat or rolling grassy land without many trees. As the wagons made their way across the plains, the tall prairie grasses hid the wagons' wheels from view. One could only see the wagons' tall, white canvas tops.

From a distance, the white tops of the wagons looked like canvas ship sails. From a distance, they looked like a fleet of ships in a sea of grass. Wagons were given the nickname "prairie schooners" or "ships of the plains" because of how they looked.

Traveling in wagons did not make for a fast or comfortable journey. Oxen, animals used to pull the wagons, walked only 1 to 2 miles (1.6 to 3.2 kilometers) per hour. Wagon trains usually traveled 10 to 15 miles (16.1 to 24 kilometers) a day. They went less in bad weather or when the ground was rough. Since the wagons were filled with supplies for the long journey, there was little room for passengers. The only passengers were very old, young, or sick. Even the person driving the wagons walked. He or she walked alongside the oxen or mules pulling the wagon.

Pioneers left messages on the trails going west. Paper messages were stuck to trees or wedged under rocks. Other messages were painted directly on rocks or skulls. One message said, "Look at this—look at this! The water here is poison, and we have lost six of our cattle. Do not let your cattle drink on this bottom."

Why Wagons Were Called Ships

After reading the story, answer the questions.
Fill in the circle next to the correct answer.

1. This story is mainly about
   - (a) prairies and schooners
   - (b) pioneers and schooners
   - (c) prairies and covered wagons
   - (d) pioneers and covered wagons

2. How many U-shaped bows was the canvas cloth stretched over to cover a wagon?
   - (a) 1 to 2
   - (b) 3 to 4
   - (c) 5 to 6
   - (d) 7 to 8

3. Think about how the word *grass* relates to *prairie*. What words relate in the same way?

grass : prairie

   - (a) ocean : sea
   - (b) fleet : wagon
   - (c) trees : forest
   - (d) plains : mountains

4. From the story, you can tell that
   - (a) it took a long time to travel west
   - (b) there was little water on the way west
   - (c) pioneers would have liked to sail to the west
   - (d) the wagons traveled the same distance every day

5. Who would most likely be a passenger on a wagon?
   - (a) Rose, a mother
   - (b) Daniel, a baby
   - (c) Molly, a six-year-old child
   - (d) Charles, a person driving the wagon

Who and Where

These are new words to practice.

Say each word 10 times.

✳ dwellings	✳ locations
✳ fronds	✳ levels
✳ furniture	✳ Seminole
✳ climate	✳ Everglades

Before or after reading the story, write one sentence that contains at least one new word.

_____

_____

_____

Who and Where

Mr. Ha said, "Class, you will be detectives today. I will give you clues. You will follow the clues to figure out who and where. The clues are about the houses the people lived in. The houses were open on all four sides. The roofs of the dwellings were made of thick, fan-shaped palm fronds, or leaves. The dwelling floors were raised more than two feet above the ground.

"Each building was only one room, but the people had several dwellings in a clearing. One building was for sleeping. Another building was for cooking and eating. Another building was for relaxing and telling stories. None of the dwellings had furniture."

Sally said, "You gave us lots of information. From the information, we know that the people had to live in a hot climate. No one could live in open-sided dwellings if they lived in a cold climate. Also, you told us their roofs were made from thick, fan-shaped palm fronds. So the people lived where these plants grow."

Alberto said, "I think the lack of furniture tells us something. Moving furniture would be a lot of work. So I think the lack of furniture tells us that these people often switched locations. Perhaps they had several camps. During different times of the year they lived at camps in different locations. The clue about the raised floors tells us something, too. It tells us that it often flooded where the dwellings were built. The floors were raised so that they would be above water when water levels rose."

Yolanda said, "We have studied how many Native Americans lived long ago. Putting all the clues together, we can tell who and where. The people are the Seminole Native Americans. The Seminole people came to live in the Florida Everglades. It is hot in the swamps of the Everglades where many palms grow. Water levels often rise. It depends on the rain. By moving to different locations, the Seminoles could find new places to plant corn, as well as follow the animals they hunted."

Who and Where

After reading the story, answer the questions.
Fill in the circle next to the correct answer.

1. What clue told the class that the people often switched locations?

   (a) the raised floors

   (b) the lack of furniture

   (c) the open-sided dwellings

   (d) the roofs made of palm fronds

2. From the story, one can tell that

   (a) palms only grow in the Everglades

   (b) all Native Americans lived in swamps

   (c) dwellings can tell one a lot about a people

   (d) people who switch locations never have furniture

3. This story is mainly about

   (a) different houses

   (b) being a detective

   (c) Seminole dwellings

   (d) Mr. Ha and his class

4. From the story, one can guess that one reason the Seminoles moved might be that

   (a) the climate was too hot

   (b) they had to get palm fronds

   (c) the water level depended on the rain

   (d) the animals they hunted did not stay in one place

5. Think about how the word *bed* relates to *furniture*. What words relate in the same way?

bed : furniture

   (a) hammer : tool

   (b) car : airplane

   (c) house : school

   (d) clue : detective

A Time to Wear a Sword

These are new words to practice.

Say each word 10 times.

* diplomat   * respect

* minister   * mistaken

* citizen   * servant

* presented   * compromise

Before or after reading the story, write one sentence that contains at least one new word.

_____

_____

_____

A Time to Wear a Sword

In 1853, James Buchanan was a diplomat. A diplomat is a person who acts for his or her country. A diplomat deals with other countries. President Pierce made Buchanan a minister. He made Buchanan his minister to Great Britain. Buchanan wanted to be a good diplomat, but he had a problem. What was the problem?

President Pierce's Secretary of State was a man named William Marcy. Marcy gave an order. All diplomats had to follow the order. The order was on dress. The order said that diplomats had to dress a certain way. How did they have to dress? They had to dress "in the simple dress of an American citizen." The order meant that Buchanan could not dress up. He had to wear ordinary clothes. He had to dress simply. He had to dress like an ordinary American citizen.

Buchanan was told something. He was told he would not be presented in the royal court. He would not be presented in the royal court if he were dressed simply. To the English, dressing simply showed something. It showed that Buchanan did not respect the Queen. Buchanan was told that if he dressed simply, he would be mistaken for a servant. Buchanan did not want to be mistaken for a servant. He wanted to show respect. How could he follow orders? How could he be a good diplomat?

Buchanan made a compromise. A compromise is a settling of an argument. It is a deal. In a compromise, both sides give up something. Each side gives up part of what it wants. The compromise was that Buchanan could wear his everyday clothes. He did not have to dress up. He could follow orders. But, Buchanan had to wear a sword. The sword was plain. It had a black handle. The plain, black-handled sword set Buchanan apart from the servants. Wearing the sword showed respect. It showed respect for the Queen.

Buchanan was our 15th president. He was the only president who never married. He became president after Pierce. He was president from 1857 to 1861. Abraham Lincoln was president after Buchanan.

A Time to Wear a Sword

**After reading the story, answer the questions.
Fill in the circle next to the correct answer.**

1. This story is mainly about
   - ⓐ how to dress
   - ⓑ showing respect
   - ⓒ a diplomat's problem
   - ⓓ Buchanan as president

2. Why did Buchanan have to wear a sword?
   - ⓐ He had to follow orders.
   - ⓑ He had to show he was a servant.
   - ⓒ He had to show respect for the Queen.
   - ⓓ He had to look like an ordinary American citizen.

3. Think about how the word *settle* relates to *argument*. What words relate in the same way?

settle : argument

   - ⓐ follow : orders
   - ⓑ dress : ordinary
   - ⓒ compromise : deal
   - ⓓ diplomat : country

4. From the story, you can tell that Buchanan
   - ⓐ was president when he was a minister
   - ⓑ was president after he was a minister
   - ⓒ was president before he was a minister
   - ⓓ was president because he was a minister

5. Who gave the order that Buchanan had to dress simply?
   - ⓐ the Queen
   - ⓑ a diplomat
   - ⓒ the president
   - ⓓ the Secretary of State

When Rivers Catch on Fire

These are new words to practice.

Say each word 10 times.

✳ pollutants	✳ sewage
✳ chemicals	✳ raw
✳ agency	✳ research
✳ environmental	✳ soil

**Before or after reading the story, write one sentence
that contains at least one new word.**

_____

_____

_____

When Rivers Catch on Fire

In 1972 a river caught on fire. It was the Cuyahoga River in Ohio. It caught on fire because it was so polluted. There were so many pollutants and chemicals in the water that the river began to burn! Fortunately, there is an agency that works to stop environmental pollution. The agency is called the Environmental Protection Agency. It is commonly known as the EPA.

The EPA is a government agency. The agency was started in 1970. Its purpose is to help keep our environment free of pollutants. It also works to clean up areas that were polluted in the past. The EPA works hard to protect our water. It works hard to keep our rivers clean. It works to keep our rivers pollution free so that they will not catch on fire.

How does the EPA do this? The EPA makes rules. Some rules are about sewage. Sewage is waste matter. It is waste matter carried off by sewers or drains. The EPA rules say that sewage cannot be raw. Raw sewage cannot be dumped into rivers or lakes. Raw sewage has to be treated first. Dangerous pollutants have to be removed.

What happens if companies or people do not follow the rules? What happens if factories dump untreated sewage into rivers or lakes? The EPA can fine companies or people. The companies or people have to pay money. Sometimes, the EPA can shut factories down. The factories cannot start up again until they obey the rules.

The EPA does research, too. Research is careful study. Some EPA research has to do with water. It has to do with water in the ground. It has to do with water trees use. EPA researchers planted trees. They planted the trees in polluted soil. The trees pulled water up into their roots. They needed the water to grow. At the same time, the trees helped clean the soil! They helped by soaking up pollutants and chemicals in the water. Still, the trees were able to grow!

When Rivers Catch on Fire

After reading the story, answer the questions.
Fill in the circle next to the correct answer.

1. If the EPA fines a company, the company has to
   - (a) pay money
   - (b) plant trees
   - (c) treat sewage
   - (d) shut down factories

2. This story is mainly about
   - (a) pollution
   - (b) a government agency
   - (c) a river that burned in Ohio
   - (d) research on trees and water

3. From the story, you can tell that
   - (a) some chemicals can burn
   - (b) all factories dump sewage into rivers
   - (c) some trees need pollutants in the soil
   - (d) all researchers work for a government agency

4. When it does research on trees planted on polluted soil, the EPA is probably least concerned with
   - (a) what trees use the most water
   - (b) what trees are the best looking
   - (c) what trees can live on the most polluted soil
   - (d) what trees are the cheapest and easiest to plant

5. Think about how the word *up* relates to *down*. What words relate in the same way?

up : down

   - (a) tree : soil
   - (b) fire : burns
   - (c) raw : treated
   - (d) study : research

The Pony Express

These are new words to practice.

Say each word 10 times.

* express   * direction

* service   * route

* delivered   * relay

* opposite   * bay

Before or after reading the story, write one sentence that contains at least one new word.

_____

_____

_____

The Pony Express

"Wanted: young, skinny, wiry fellows not over 18. Must be expert riders, willing to risk death daily. Orphans preferred. Wages $25 a week." When this ad was placed in newspapers, people responded quickly. Jobs were usually filled in only one or two days! What was the ad for? What were these jobs that people really wanted?

The ad was for the Pony Express. The Pony Express was a mail service. It carried mail between Saint Joseph, Missouri, and San Francisco, California. This was a distance of nearly 2,000 miles (3,219 km). At the time of the Pony Express, there were no railroads or good roads between Missouri and California. This made mail service very slow. It could take months for a letter to be delivered. Often, letters never arrived.

The Pony Express changed this. It got the mail delivered fast! How fast? Its goal was just 10 days! How could mail be delivered so quickly? Riders rode day and night, racing in opposite directions. Each rider's route was about 100 miles (161 km) long. Relay stations lay along the route about every 10 miles (16 km).

When a rider neared a relay station, he would blow a horn. This would alert the stationmaster that a fresh horse should be ready and waiting to go. This was important, as a rider was given only two minutes to switch horses. At the end of his route, the rider would eat and rest at a "home" station. When the mail came through from the opposite direction, he would race back along his route.

Adventure came with the job. One night a rider was followed by a pack of wolves. The rider had lent his gun to another rider just that day. How did the rider keep the wolves at bay? The rider blew his horn. The sound kept the wolves at bay. The rider blew his horn until he was safe at the next station. The Pony Express's first run was on April 3, 1860. It ended October 26, 1861. This was two days after the western and eastern states were connected by telegraph.

The Pony Express

After reading the story, answer the questions.
Fill in the circle next to the correct answer.

1. How much time was a rider given to switch to a fresh horse?

   ⓐ one minute

   ⓑ two minutes

   ⓒ 10 minutes

   ⓓ 25 minutes

2. This story is mainly about

   ⓐ the Pony Express

   ⓑ mail service today

   ⓒ how the Pony Express got riders

   ⓓ the time it takes mail to be delivered

3. When something is kept at bay, it is kept

   ⓐ safe

   ⓑ away

   ⓒ close

   ⓓ connected

4. What might be one reason the Pony Express ended?

   ⓐ a road had been made for telegraph poles

   ⓑ it took months for a letter to be delivered

   ⓒ news could be delivered faster by telegraph

   ⓓ riding for the Pony Express was too dangerous

5. Think about how the word *switch* relates to *change*. What words relate in the same way?

switch : change

   ⓐ blow : horn

   ⓑ fresh : tired

   ⓒ ready : waiting

   ⓓ respond : answer

Losing a Year for a Day

These are new words to practice.

Say each word 10 times.

✳ international	✳ Greenwich
✳ hypothetical	✳ England
✳ meridian	✳ schedule
✳ agreement	✳ zone

Before or after reading the story, write one sentence that contains at least one new word.

_____

_____

_____

Losing a Year for a Day

Debra was 10 years old. She had her birthday on May 1st. Then, she went back to being nine years old. After a day, she was 10 years old again. Debra lost a year for a day. She had two birthdays. How was it possible?

Debra crossed the International Date Line. The International Date Line is a hypothetical line. Something hypothetical is supposed. The date line is a supposed line. It is not real. It runs pretty much with the meridian 180° from Greenwich, England. The Date Line is fixed. It is fixed by international agreement. It is fixed as the place where each calendar day first begins.

Debra crossed the line going east. If one crosses the line going east, one sets one's calendar back one day. Debra had two birthdays by being west of the date line on her birthday, May 1st. Then, Debra crossed the line going east. East of the line, the date was not May 1st. It was April 30th. Debra was no longer ten. She was nine again! She remained nine until it was May 1st on the eastern side of the date line.

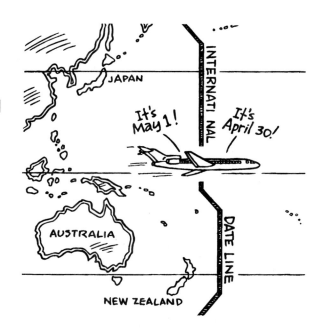

Why is there a date line? Why is there international agreement about a hypothetical line? Think about business. Think about schedules. A schedule is a timetable. The world would be a very confusing place if everyone had their own time. What if a plane left and landed on its own time? How would people know when it was arriving or leaving local time? Schedules would be impossible to work out!

In 1884, nations agreed to divide the world into 24 time zones. Twelve time zones are east of Greenwich. Twelve time zones are west of Greenwich. There is one hour of time difference between each zone. Greenwich, England was chosen as "starting time" because most sailors around the world already used Greenwich as their prime meridian, or line of 0 degrees longitude on their maps. The date line does not run exactly at the 180° meridian because it jogs around some countries the line would divide.

Losing a Year for a Day

After reading the story, answer the questions.
Fill in the circle next to the correct answer.

1. How many time zones are there?
   - ⓐ 10
   - ⓑ 12
   - ⓒ 24
   - ⓓ 180

2. This story is mainly about
   - ⓐ the starting point
   - ⓑ a hypothetical line
   - ⓒ Debra's two birthdays
   - ⓓ birthdays around the world

3. If one traveled westward over the International Date Line, one would
   - ⓐ move one's calendar back one day
   - ⓑ move one's calendar ahead one day
   - ⓒ keep one's calendar at the same day
   - ⓓ keep one's calendar in the same time zone

4. What is not true about the International Date Line?
   - ⓐ It is a hypothetical line.
   - ⓑ It was agreed upon in 1884.
   - ⓒ It runs along the line of 0° latitude.
   - ⓓ It jogs around some countries it would divide.

5. Think about how the word *clock* relates to *time*. What words relate in the same way?

clock : time

   - ⓐ zone : hour
   - ⓑ east : west
   - ⓒ start : begin
   - ⓓ calendar : day

Seven Words

These are new words to practice.

Say each word 10 times.

* Alabama   * arrested

* attention   * notices

* equally   * boycott

* passengers   * companies

Before or after reading the story, write one sentence that contains at least one new word.

_____

_____

_____

Seven Words

In 1955, Montgomery, Alabama, was called "the Walking City." This was because of seven words. The seven words were, "Please stay off all buses on Monday." People paid attention to the words. On Monday, the buses were empty. Instead of taking the bus, people walked to school and work. What was going on? What turned Montgomery, Alabama, into a "walking city"?

Long ago, people of different colors were not treated equally. They were not treated fairly. In Montgomery, black passengers had to sit in the back of the bus. They could not sit in the front even if the bus was crowded and there were no white passengers on the bus! Black people were not treated equally, but they had to pay the same fare. They had to pay the same amount to ride the bus as white people.

One day, a black woman named Rosa Parks sat down. When a white man wanted to sit in her row, she was ordered to the back of the bus. Parks would not give up her seat. She was tired of being treated unfairly. She was tired of being treated as if her skin color made her less of a person. Parks was arrested.

When people heard about Parks being arrested, they quickly printed up some notices. They sent the notices out. The notice told about Parks's arrest. It asked people to boycott the buses. A boycott is when people refuse to buy, sell, or use something. A bus boycott meant that no one should ride or use the bus. The notice said, "Please stay off all buses on Monday."

People paid attention to the notices. On Monday, the buses were empty. People decided to continue the boycott until all passengers were treated the same. Soon, Montgomery became "The Walking City" because everyone was walking. People walked in the hot, blazing sun. They walked in the cold, drizzling rain. They walked for over a year. The bus companies lost a lot of money. The boycott ended when the bus companies said they would treat all passengers fairly.

Seven Words

**After reading the story, answer the questions.
Fill in the circle next to the correct answer.**

1. This story is mainly about
   - (a) walking in Montgomery, Alabama
   - (b) sitting in the back of the bus
   - (c) words on notices that were handed out
   - (d) a bus boycott and being treated equally

2. Why was Montgomery called "the Walking City"?
   - (a) Passengers were treated unfairly.
   - (b) People walked instead of riding the bus.
   - (c) Black passengers had to sit in the back of the bus.
   - (d) Bus passengers of different colors had to pay the same fares.

3. People boycotted the buses because
   - (a) they liked to walk
   - (b) they did not want to be arrested
   - (c) they wanted to pay a different fare
   - (d) they wanted all passengers to be treated the same

4. Think about how the word *equal* relates to *unfair*. What words relate in the same way?

equal : unfair

   - (a) money : fare
   - (b) cold : drizzling
   - (c) boycotted : used
   - (d) passenger : rider

5. Which answer lists what happened in the story in the right order?
   - (a) Parks is arrested, notices are handed out, a boycott starts
   - (b) notices are handed out, a boycott starts, Parks is arrested
   - (c) Parks is arrested, a boycott starts, Parks refuses to give up her seat
   - (d) Parks refuses to give up her seat, a boycott starts, Parks is arrested

Old Ironsides

These are new words to practice.

Say each word 10 times.

* Constitution	* canvas
* launched	* hammocks
* document	* stow
* berth deck	* spar deck

Before or after reading the story, write one sentence that contains at least one new word.

_____

_____

_____

Old Ironsides

The U.S.S. *Constitution* was launched in 1797. The ship was named after the Constitution of the United States. The Constitution is a document, or paper. This document is the basis of our government. When the *Constitution* was launched, it became the third ship in the United States Navy. The ship was soon called another name. It became known as Old Ironsides.

The name came about during the War of 1812. The War of 1812 was between the United States and Britain. Part of the war was over shipping rights. The United States did not want the British taking over its ships and forcing sailors into the British navy. In one battle, the *Constitution* faced the H.M.S. *Guerrière*. The *Guerrière* shot cannonballs at the *Constitution*.

Some cannonballs caused damage. But many other cannonballs simply bounced. They bounced off the thick wooden ship. When this happened, a sailor called out, "Huzzah! Her sides are made of iron!" The *Constitution* shot its own guns. The *Guerrière* was quickly sunk. The *Constitution* became known as Old Ironsides.

Sailors on Old Ironsides slept on the berth deck. The berth deck had low ceilings. The men had to be careful not to bang their heads on the low ceilings. The men slept in hammocks. The hammocks were made of canvas, a strong, heavy cloth. The canvas hammocks were hung from hooks. The men slept crowded together. In the morning, the sailors had just 12 minutes to dress, roll and stow their hammocks on the top spar deck, and report for duty.

With such a short time, why did the men have to stow their hammocks on the spar deck? Why couldn't the hammocks be left hanging? First, space on the berth deck was needed. Wounded sailors were treated here during battle. Second, the stowed hammocks helped protect the sailors. The tightly-rolled hammocks were piled against the spar deck side. They were held down with a net. The hammocks made it harder for enemy gunmen to shoot at the crew. Also, when cannonballs hit the ship, the hammocks absorbed flying splinters.

Old Ironsides

After reading the story, answer the questions.
Fill in the circle next to the correct answer.

1. How many minutes were sailors given to report for duty in the morning?
   - (a) 10
   - (b) 12
   - (c) 14
   - (d) 16

2. This story is mainly about
   - (a) the War of 1812
   - (b) a ship in the United States Navy
   - (c) how sailors slept on Old Ironsides
   - (d) a battle between the *Constitution* and the *Guerrière*

3. What is not true about the *Constitution*?
   - (a) It was made of iron.
   - (b) It was launched in 1797.
   - (c) It had more than one deck.
   - (d) It was the third ship in the United States Navy.

4. Which word best fits in the blank? "Summer had come! It was time to _____ away our winter clothes."
   - (a) stow
   - (b) launch
   - (c) canvas
   - (d) protect

5. Think about how the term *berth deck* relates to *spar deck*. What words relate in the same way?

berth deck : spar deck

   - (a) high : low
   - (b) on : under
   - (c) top : bottom
   - (d) below : above

A Palindrome
and a President

These are new words to practice.
Say each word 10 times.

* palindrome   * Panama

* phrase   * Columbia

* famous   * revolt

* canal   * preserved

Before or after reading the story, write one sentence that contains at least one new word.

_____

_____

_____

A Palindrome and a President

A palindrome is a word or a phrase. A palindrome can be read front to back. It can be read back to front. No matter how a palindrome is read, it is the same. Look at the words *noon* and *racecar*. You can read *noon* and *racecar* from left to right. You can read them right to left. The letters spell the same words either way.

One palindrome is very famous. It is about a president. The palindrome goes like this: *A man, a plan, a canal, Panama!* *A man, a plan, a canal, Panama!* can be read front to back. It can be read back to front. Both ways, the letters spell out the same phrase. This palindrome was written about Theodore Roosevelt. Theodore Roosevelt was known as Teddy Roosevelt. (Our toy teddy bears were also named after Roosevelt.)

Roosevelt was born in 1858. He was our 26th president. He was president from 1901 to 1909. When Roosevelt was president, he wanted a canal built. He wanted a canal that big ships could go through. He wanted a canal built in Panama. It would cut across Central America. This way, ships could travel to and from the Pacific and Atlantic oceans without going around South America.

Theodore Roosevelt

At that time, Panama was a part of Colombia. Roosevelt offered to buy land from Colombia. He offered a price. Colombia would not agree. It wanted a higher price. Then, people in Panama had a revolt. They revolted against Colombia. Roosevelt recognized Panama as a new country. He sent warships to protect it. The new country of Panama then sold Roosevelt land. It agreed to Roosevelt's price. The man Roosevelt had a plan. His plan was for a canal in Panama. He made his plan work by getting land in Panama.

Roosevelt is famous for land in another way. He believed some land should be preserved. It should be protected. It should be kept safe from harm or damage. As president, Roosevelt took 125 million acres of public land. He preserved it in national forests.

A Palindrome and a President

After reading the story, answer the questions.
Fill in the circle next to the correct answer.

1. This story is mainly about
   - (a) a man and land
   - (b) a man who built a canal
   - (c) a man who became president
   - (d) a man with a plan and a palindrome

2. The Panama Canal cuts across Central America so that ships can travel to and from
   - (a) the Pacific and Indian oceans
   - (b) the Atlantic and Indian oceans
   - (c) the Atlantic and Pacific oceans
   - (d) the Pacific and South American oceans

3. When something is protected and kept safe from harm, it is
   - (a) famous
   - (b) damaged
   - (c) revolted
   - (d) preserved

4. Think about how the word *Panama* relates to *country*. What words relate in the same way?

   Panama : country

   - (a) canal : land
   - (b) teddy bear : toy
   - (c) Colombia : price
   - (d) national forest : safe

5. Which word is not a palindrome?
   - (a) eye
   - (b) noon
   - (c) seas
   - (d) madam

A Stuffed Hero and Ordinary Shoes

These are new words to practice.

Say each word 10 times.

* Smithsonian   * ordinary

* complex   * preserver

* galleries   * ether

* pigeon   * inhaler

Before or after reading the story, write one sentence that contains at least one new word.

_____

_____

_____

A Stuffed Hero and Ordinary Shoes

Mr. Young's class went on a field trip. The field trip was to the Smithsonian. The Smithsonian was started in 1846. It is in Washington D.C. It is a vast complex. Something vast is big. Something complex is made up of several different things. The Smithsonian is made up of several museums and galleries. Many different objects are in the museums. Many different pictures are in the galleries. The objects and pictures are from America's past.

Mr. Young let his class explore the vast complex. He said each student had to find a favorite thing. Joe said, "I liked a stuffed hero. The hero was a bird. The bird was a carrier pigeon. The carrier pigeon was a soldier. He was a soldier in World War I. He carried messages during the war. He was wounded in action. He was a real hero."

Ella said, "I liked some shoes. The shoes were ordinary, but the shoes had been worn on a march. The march was in 1965. The march was 54 miles (86.4 kilometers) long. The march was for equal voting rights. The marchers wanted equal voting rights for people of all colors. The shoes made me think about our history. The shoes made me think about how ordinary people have fought for equal voting rights."

Mori said, "I liked the life preserver. An explorer wore the life preserver. The explorer was John Powell. Powell wore the preserver when he explored the Green and Colorado Rivers. He wore it in 1869. Some words were written on the preserver. The words said, 'I can't talk or I would tell you some queer things. I have been under the water many times and saved one Brave Man's life more times than one.'"

Hector said, "I liked seeing an invention. The invention put people to sleep. The invention made it so people could be asleep when they were operated on. The invention was called an ether inhaler. When people inhaled (breathed in) ether, they fell asleep. William T.G. Morton invented the ether inhaler. He invented it around 1846."

A Stuffed Hero and Ordinary Shoes

After reading the story, answer the questions.
Fill in the circle next to the correct answer.

1. Which student liked the carrier pigeon?

   (a) Joe

   (b) Mori

   (c) Ella

   (d) Hector

2. This story is mainly about

   (a) what students like about museums

   (b) the Smithsonian and objects in it

   (c) a stuffed hero and ordinary shoes

   (d) Mr. Young's field trip to America's past

3. From the story, you can tell that

   (a) Morton needed to be operated on

   (b) Powell sometimes fell in the water

   (c) the carrier pigeon died around 1846

   (d) only ordinary things are in the Smithsonian

4. Which word best fills in the blank? "This mall has a lot of stores. It is a big _____."

   (a) museum

   (b) inhaler

   (c) complex

   (d) gallery

5. Think about how the word *march* relates to *walk*. What words relate in the same way?

   march : walk

   (a) explore : like

   (b) hero : ordinary

   (c) museum : object

   (d) inhale : breathe

Buffalo Soldiers

These are new words to practice.

Say each word 10 times.

* vacation

* buffalo

* soldiers

* allowed

* territory

* wilderness

* telegraph

* calvary

Before or after reading the story, write one sentence that contains at least one new word.

_____

_____

_____

Buffalo Soldiers

A vacation is a time to rest. How many days of vacation were buffalo soldiers allowed? The soldiers were allowed only two days! They were given only two rest days all year. One vacation day was July 4. The other rest day was December 25. Except for those two days, buffalo soldiers worked seven days a week. They worked 12 months a year.

The work they did was hard. They explored new territory. The territory was in the West. It was unexplored wilderness. They built roads. The roads they built were the first roads. The roads were in the wilderness. They laid telegraph lines. The telegraph lines were laid across rough and dangerous lands.

They traveled in deserts. They found water holes in the deserts. They told new settlers where the water holes were. They built settlements. A settlement is a place where people come to live. They guarded the mail. They kept the men carrying the mail safe from dangerous attacks. The buffalo soldiers worked hard. They did not quit. They did not run away. Fewer buffalo soldiers ran away than any other cavalry group in the army. Just who were the buffalo soldiers?

Buffalo soldiers were soldiers in the United States Army. They were all African Americans. Many of them had fought in the Civil War. They had fought in the Union Army. Buffalo soldiers served in the western part of the United States. They served from 1867 to about 1896. They made up the 9th and 10th Cavalries. The Native Americans named them. The Native Americans called the men of the 9th and 10th Cavalries buffalo soldiers.

At that time, black and white soldiers were separated. They did not fight alongside each other. They were not allowed to. They did not work together. They were not allowed to. Some white army officers would not work with African American soldiers. They refused. Today, we know that is wrong. Today, soldiers of all colors work together. Army leaders are of all colors. It is one army working all together.

Buffalo Soldiers

After reading the story, answer the questions.
Fill in the circle next to the correct answer.

1. This story is mainly about
   - (a) vacation time
   - (b) the army working together
   - (c) soldiers serving in the West
   - (d) soldiers in the 9th and 10th Cavalries

2. How long did buffalo soldiers serve?
   - (a) 1864 to about 1894
   - (b) 1865 to about 1894
   - (c) 1866 to about 1896
   - (d) 1867 to about 1896

3. Very few buffalo soldiers
   - (a) ran away
   - (b) guarded the mail
   - (c) built settlements
   - (d) laid telegraph lines

4. Think about how the word *day* relates to *week*. What words relate in the same way?

day : week

   - (a) month : year
   - (b) seven : twelve
   - (c) work : vacation
   - (d) separated : alongside

5. Which word best fits in the blank? "We cannot swim today. It is not _____."
   - (a) served
   - (b) allowed
   - (c) separated
   - (d) unexplored

Imaginary Lines and the World's Smallest Bird

These are new words to practice.

Say each word 10 times.

⁎ imaginary	⁎ longitude
⁎ measurements	⁎ prime
⁎ latitude	⁎ meridian
⁎ equator	⁎ intersect

Before or after reading the story, write one sentence that contains at least one new word.

_____

_____

_____

Imaginary Lines and the World's Smallest Bird

Tim said, "I am thinking of a country. The smallest bird in the world lives in this country. How small is the bird? It is only 2 inches (5 centimeters) long, and half of that is the beak and tail! I will not tell you the name of the country, but using imaginary lines you can find it."

Rose said, "I know what those lines are. You are going to give me two measurements. The measurements will be where the country falls on two imaginary lines. One of the imaginary lines will be the latitude line. The latitude lines are the east-west lines on maps. Latitude lines are above and below the equator. The equator is another imaginary line. It goes around the middle of the Earth. It divides the Earth into two halves."

"The imaginary lines are measured in degrees," Tim said. "The equator is the 0° line. Latitude lines are measured in degrees north and south of the equator. The North Pole has a latitude of 90 degrees north. The South Pole has a latitude of 90 degrees south. The country I am thinking of is 22 degrees north of the equator. This means it is between the North Pole and the equator. But you need to know more. You need to know the longitude measurement.

"Longitude lines run north-south. The starting point is the 0° longitude mark. It is called the prime meridian. The prime meridian runs from the North Pole to the South Pole. It runs through Greenwich, England. It divides the world into east and west. The country I am thinking of is 80 degrees west of the prime meridian."

Rose cried, "I can figure it out! I just have to find where the lines of latitude and longitude intersect, or cross. I can find my place anywhere in the world as long as I know where the imaginary lines intersect." What country lies 22° north of the equator and 80° west of the prime meridian? Cuba! Cuba is an island. The world's smallest bird lives on the island country of Cuba.

Imaginary Lines and the World's Smallest Bird

After reading the story, answer the questions.
Fill in the circle next to the correct answer.

1. This story is mainly about
   - (a) latitude
   - (b) Tim and Rose
   - (c) imaginary lines
   - (d) the world's smallest bird

2. Lines of latitude
   - (a) run east-west on maps
   - (b) run north-south on maps
   - (c) are east or west of the equator
   - (d) are north or south of the prime meridian

3. Think about how the word *prime meridian* relates to *longitude*. What words relate in the same way?

   | prime meridian : longitude |

   - (a) imaginary : line
   - (b) equator : latitude
   - (c) measurement : degrees
   - (d) North Pole : South Pole

4. When two lines intersect, they
   - (a) cross
   - (b) divide
   - (c) are imaginary
   - (d) are measured in degrees

5. What is *not* true about the prime meridian?
   - (a) It is an imaginary line.
   - (b) It is the 0 degree longitude mark.
   - (c) It runs through Greenwich, England.
   - (d) It is where the world's smallest bird lives.

Sunken Treasure

These are new words to practice.

Say each word 10 times.

* cargo   * salvage

* wreckage   * efforts

* visible   * structure

* depth   * documents

Before or after reading the story, write one sentence that contains at least one new word.

_____

_____

_____

Sunken Treasure

A Spanish ship sank in 1622. It broke up on a coral reef. It was blown onto the reef by hurricane winds. The ship was filled with valuable cargo worth hundreds of millions of dollars. It carried gold, silver, and jewels. The treasure had come from Spain's colonies in the New World. Its valuable cargo was intended for the King of Spain. The ship was called the *Atocha*. 260 people drowned. Only five survivors were pulled from the wreckage.

One of *Atocha's* masts was visible sticking out of the water. The wreck was resting at a depth of 55 feet (16.8 meters). Divers were sent down. They could not salvage, or save, the cargo. This was because the depth was the limit for their lungs. Plus, the ship's hatches were sealed. Then, another hurricane struck. After the storm, the mast and wreckage close to the surface was no longer visible.

The ship was harder to find without the mast, but the king still wanted his treasure salvaged. Trained pearl divers were sent for. The pearl divers were excellent divers, but they were able to recover only a small amount of silver. The wreck became covered in sand. Still, salvage efforts continued.

In 1626, a slave was put in a diving bell. The diving bell was a bell-shaped structure. The structure was open to the water at the bottom. Air was pumped into it from a surface hose. The air pressure kept the bell from filling up with water. The slave found one wreck. It was not the *Atocha*.

Hope was gone by 1676, but treasure hunters still continued their efforts. Treasure hunter Mel Fisher finally found the *Atocha* on July 20, 1985. How did Fisher accomplish what no one else could? Fisher had good scuba-diving equipment. He also had new information. The information came from old documents. The documents showed that treasure hunters had been searching in the wrong place for hundreds of years! Island names had been changed on old documents and maps by mistake! The *Atocha* was over 100 miles from where it was thought to be!

124

Sunken Treasure

After reading the story, answer the questions.
Fill in the circle next to the correct answer.

1. This story is mainly about
   - (a) finding treasure
   - (b) a valuable treasure
   - (c) recovering treasure
   - (d) how a treasure was lost

2. How many years after hope was gone was the *Atocha* found?
   - (a) 309
   - (b) 359
   - (c) 363
   - (d) 379

3. Where was the surface hose that was used to pump air into the diving bell most probably located?
   - (a) on a ship that was sailing to Spain
   - (b) on a ship with good scuba diving equipment
   - (c) on a ship that was not in the way of hurricane winds
   - (d) on a ship that rested above where the bell was sent down

4. Think about how the word *close* relates to *far*. What words relate in the same way?

   close : far

   - (a) recover : save
   - (b) salvage : wreck
   - (c) documents : paper
   - (d) information : news

5. If the ship sunk today at the same depth, most likely
   - (a) the mast would not remain visible
   - (b) the treasure would not need to be salvaged
   - (c) trained pearl divers would be sent to search for the treasure
   - (d) the treasure would be recovered quickly because of scuba equipment

What the Numbers Tell

These are new words to practice.

Say each word 10 times.

✳ interstate	✳ construction
✳ topic	✳ digits
✳ system	✳ direction
✳ network	✳ increase

Before or after reading the story, write one sentence that contains at least one new word.

_____

_____

_____

What the Numbers Tell

Ty did not want to do a history report. Ty said he liked math better than history. "I like numbers," Ty said. "Numbers can tell us a lot." Ms. Evans laughed. She told Ty that he could do a report on the history of the interstate highways in the United States. Ty did not like the topic, but he had no choice. He had to report on the topic Ms. Evans gave him.

Ty found out that the interstate highway system is a network. It is a network of highways that link the states together. Construction began in 1956. Construction took 37 years. The last link was completed in 1993. The system is 42,800 miles (68,865 kilometers) long.

As Ty read more, he started to laugh. Now he knew why Ms. Evans had given him the topic. Numbers told him a lot about the interstate system! Ty could look at any interstate highway with one or two digits and say what direction it went. Odd-numbered interstates with one or two digits run north to south. I-5 and I-95 run north to south. The numbers increase as one travels from the West Coast to the East Coast. So I-5 is in the west, and I-95 is in the east.

Even-numbered interstates run east to west. I-10 and I-94 run east to west. The numbers increase as one travels from the south to the north. So I-10 is in the south. I-94 is in the north. Not all interstates go exactly north to south or east to west. Those interstates were given numbers based on the road's general direction.

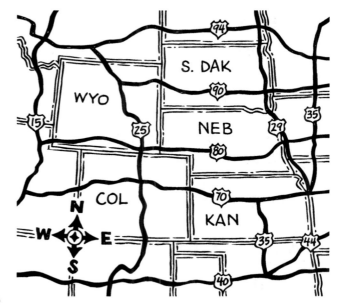

Numbers told Ty what interstate highways connect to other major highways. Interstates with three digits connect to other major highways. If the first digit of the number is even, the interstate highway connects to another interstate at both ends. These highways often loop around a city. If the first digit of the number starts with an odd digit, the interstate highway connects to another interstate at only one end. These highways often go into a city.

What the Numbers Tell

**After reading the story, answer the questions.
Fill in the circle next to the correct answer.**

1. This story is mainly about
   - (a) numbers
   - (b) directions
   - (c) a history topic
   - (d) interstate highways

2. The interstate highway I-65
   - (a) runs east to west
   - (b) runs north to south
   - (c) connects to another interstate at one end
   - (d) connects to another interstate at both ends

3. One state has three interstate highways. It is the only state whose highways are not linked to other state highways. This state is most likely
   - (a) Hawaii
   - (b) Maryland
   - (c) California
   - (d) West Virginia

4. Think about how the word *odd* relates to *even*. What words relate in the same way?

odd : even

   - (a) one : three
   - (b) three : one
   - (c) two : three
   - (d) three : two

5. If one wanted to go from the West Coast to the East Coast, one should most probably take
   - (a) I-5
   - (b) I-15
   - (c) I-40
   - (d) I-77

Tricked into Eating Salted Cabbage

These are new words to practice.

Say each word 10 times.

* navigation   * resisted

* voyages   * sauerkraut

* scurvy   * announced

* local   * superior

Before or after reading the story, write one sentence that contains at least one new word.

_____

_____

_____

Tricked into Eating Salted Cabbage

Captain James Cook was an English explorer. Born in 1728, he was the son of a poor farm worker. He went to school for only a few years. At age 17, Cook shipped aboard a coal ship. He learned how to sail by working. At night, he studied sailing charts and navigation. At age 27, he joined Great Britain's Royal Navy. He quickly rose through the ranks.

Cook made three great sea voyages. He traveled to Australia and New Zealand. He visited many islands, including Tahiti and Hawaii. He traveled around South America and up the North American coast. In all, Cook visited six continents. He also sailed closer to Antarctica than anyone had before.

Cook became famous for his navigation skills. The maps and charts he made were accurate and well done. He also became famous because he kept his men healthy. Before, it was common on long voyages for entire crews to weaken and die. We know today why the sailors became unhealthy. They had scurvy. Scurvy is a disease caused from a lack of vitamin C. Vitamin C is found in fruits and other fresh foods.

Cook would always stock up on fresh local foods, no matter how strange they seemed. He did not know why, but he had noticed that fresh foods seemed to keep scurvy at bay. Cook would make his men try the local foods, but sometimes they resisted. One time, Cook wanted his men to eat sauerkraut. Sauerkraut is made of cabbage. The cabbage has been chopped, salted, and allowed to turn sour in its own juice. Cook's men resisted eating the sauerkraut. It was too strange.

Cook was clever. He tricked his men. He announced that sauerkraut was only being served to the officers. Cook wrote in his journal that when sailors "see their Superiors set a value upon it, it becomes the finest stuff in the world." As Cook predicted, his sailors soon saw sauerkraut as the "finest stuff." The sailors no longer resisted sauerkraut. In fact, they announced that they wanted to eat it along with their superior officers!

Tricked into Eating Salted Cabbage

After reading the story, answer the questions.
Fill in the circle next to the correct answer.

1. This story is mainly about
   - (a) where Cook went
   - (b) what sauerkraut is
   - (c) scurvy and vitamin C
   - (d) Cook and what he was famous for

2. What is a local food?
   - (a) a food that is fresh
   - (b) a food that keeps scurvy at bay
   - (c) a food that is grown or made close by
   - (d) a food that is chopped, salted, and allowed to sour in its own juice

3. Think about how the word *healthy* relates to *well*. What words relate in the same way?

healthy : well

   - (a) officer : crew
   - (b) famous : known
   - (c) accurate : value
   - (d) cabbage : sauerkraut

4. Cook did not go to
   - (a) Hawaii
   - (b) Australia
   - (c) Antarctica
   - (d) New Zealand

5. When Cook and his officers ate sauerkraut, they were
   - (a) showing that sauerkraut had value
   - (b) announcing that sauerkraut stopped scurvy
   - (c) not sure how long the sauerkraut would last
   - (d) getting ready to make the men eat sauerkraut

Nurse on the Battlefield

These are new words to practice.

Say each word 10 times.

* Civil War   * patients

* operating   * desperate

* surgeons   * battlefield

* chloroform   * organization

Before or after reading the story, write one sentence that contains at least one new word.

_____

_____

_____

Nurse on the Battlefield

Clara Barton listened. She listened to the sounds of gunfire. The heaviest gunfire came from the right of camp. This meant that the heaviest fighting was going on to the right of camp. So what did Barton do? She did not drive away from the heaviest fighting to safety. Instead, she drove her wagon into the cover of a cornfield. As bullets whistled overhead, she pressed forward. She went to where she was needed most.

At a clearing, Barton found over 300 wounded Civil War soldiers. The wounded soldiers were crying out in pain. Many were badly injured. Barton quickly went to where the doctors were operating. The surgeons had nothing but their instruments. The only medicine they had was the little chloroform they had brought in their pockets. Chloroform was a drug. Surgeons gave it to their patients to put them to sleep before operating.

With only instruments, how were the doctors bandaging their patients? The doctors were using what they had. They were using green corn husks. Barton's arrival was a tremendous help to the doctors desperate for supplies. Barton brought food. She brought medicine. She brought desperately needed bandages.

Barton was born on December 25, 1821. She was born in North Oxford, Massachusetts. When she was a little girl, her brother became very ill. She nursed her brother for two years. Later, she started teaching. Wanting to help children in need, she started a free public school in New Jersey. Next, she took a job in Washington, D.C. Then, in 1861, the Civil War started.

No one was nursing the soldiers. Many soldiers were dying on the battlefield. They died waiting for medical attention. Barton stepped in. At that time, women were not allowed near battlefields. Barton did not care. She knew that help was needed. During the war, Barton helped many men. After the war, she started the American Red Cross. The Red Cross is an organization. The organization helps people in times of need. All her life, Barton worked to take care of those in need.

Nurse on the Battlefield

After reading the story, answer the questions.
Fill in the circle next to the correct answer.

1. What were the surgeons using to bandage their patients?

   (a) medicine

   (b) chloroform

   (c) corn husks

   (d) instruments

2. Why would Barton know that she was needed most where the gunfire sounded the heaviest?

   (a) More gunfire meant the battle was ending.

   (b) More gunfire meant men were more likely to be wounded.

   (c) More gunfire meant women would not be on the battlefield.

   (d) More gunfire meant the doctors would have nothing but their instruments.

3. This story is mainly about

   (a) Clara Barton

   (b) the Civil War

   (c) the Red Cross

   (d) wounded soldiers

4. When did Barton start a public school for children in need?

   (a) after the Civil War

   (b) after she started the Red Cross

   (c) after she worked in Washington, D.C.

   (d) after she nursed her brother for two years

5. Think about how the word *chloroform* relates to *drug*. What words relate in the same way?

chloroform : drug

   (a) nurse : helps

   (b) surgeon : doctor

   (c) battlefield : wounded

   (d) organization : Red Cross

New Words

Coffin's House

These are new words to practice.

Say each word 10 times.

* constructed   * separated

* materials   * network

* labor   * passengers

* eaves   * stations

Before or after reading the story, write one sentence that contains at least one new word.

_____

_____

_____

Coffin's House

Levi Coffin needed a bigger house. When his new house was constructed, Coffin had it built a certain way. First, Coffin made sure that none of the materials came from slave labor. Second, he had a well room inside the house. The well room was built next to the basement kitchen. Third, Coffin had a long, windowless room built under the eaves, or roof edges. The room was constructed so cleverly that no one looking at the house from the outside could tell it was there. Inside, its tiny door was hidden behind a bed. Why?

Coffin was born in 1798. This was a time when slavery was allowed in some parts of the United States. Coffin knew that slavery was wrong. No human being should own another. Coffin saw slaves sold and separated from their families. Coffin saw slaves beaten and burned. He thought about how he would feel if it happened to him. He would not want to be separated from his family. He would not want to be beaten or burned.

Coffin worked on the "Underground Railroad" because of his feelings about slavery. The "Underground Railroad" had no cars or rails. Still, slaves rode it. The "Underground Railroad" was the name given to a network of people who worked together. All the people helped slaves escape north to freedom. The escaping slaves were "passengers." "Conductors" helped lead or take slaves to "stations" along the network. The "stations" were safe houses.

Coffin's house was one of the railroad's "Grand Central Stations." As Coffin said, "There was no lack of passengers." Coffin was thinking of "passengers" when he had his house constructed. He did not want material that came from slave labor. Paying for materials made with slave labor would support slavery.

Coffin knew passengers would need food and water. The well room was inside so that no attention was brought to how much water was drawn from the well. The basement kitchen meant that activity there was hidden. The secret room under the eaves was a place where slaves could hide if the house was searched.

Coffin's House

After reading the story, answer the questions.
Fill in the circle next to the correct answer.

1. This story is mainly about
   - (a) a railroad
   - (b) escaping slaves
   - (c) a man and his safe house
   - (d) constructing the "Underground Railroad"

2. The "Underground Railroad" was
   - (a) a network of people
   - (b) a railroad under the ground
   - (c) a train with cars for slaves
   - (d) a railroad with very few passengers

3. Think about how the word *hidden* relates to *seen*. What words relate in the same way.

hidden : seen

   - (a) roof : eaves
   - (b) construct : build
   - (c) slave : passenger
   - (d) together : separated

4. Which word best fits in the blank? "We _____ hard to get the job done."
   - (a) labored
   - (b) separated
   - (c) encouraged
   - (d) constructed

5. What might be one reason Coffin's house was called a "Grand Central Station"?
   - (a) It had a secret room.
   - (b) Slaves did not help build it.
   - (c) A lot of passengers stopped there.
   - (d) It had a well room inside the house.

A Dream of Flying

These are new words to practice.

Say each word 10 times.

* cockpit	* aviator
* strained	* propeller
* plummeted	* license
* certain	* instructor

Before or after reading the story, write one sentence that contains at least one new word.

_____

_____

_____

A Dream of Flying

Bessie Coleman was high in the air. Her scarf streamed behind her as she piloted her biplane from its open cockpit. Pulling back on the control stick, she aimed the plane skyward. She flew skyward, even as the engine strained. High in the sky, the straining engine suddenly died. The plane plummeted. When something plummets, it falls straight down. The crowd below fell silent. They were certain Coleman was plummeting to her death.

Death seemed certain, but Coleman was a skilled aviator. She was an excellent pilot. She knew how to thrill the crowd. Coleman allowed the air rushing over the propeller to kick the engine back to life. Then, Coleman quickly pulled back on the control stick. She brought the plane out of its dive. She saved herself in the nick of time. The crowd was thrilled.

Coleman received her pilot's license on June 15, 1921. She was the first woman of African American and Native American descent to do so. Becoming a licensed aviator was no easy matter. Coleman grew up in Texas. Her family was very poor. Coleman picked cotton and worked as a maid. Often, she missed school because she had to take care of her three younger sisters while her mother worked.

Despite being poor and having to work hard, Coleman never gave up her dream to fly. She worked for years, saving money. No one in the United States would teach Coleman how to fly because of her color. Coleman did not let this stop her. She learned French and moved to France.

In France, Coleman sat behind her instructor in an open cockpit. Both she and her instructor had a set of controls—a stick and a rudder bar under their feet. The controls could be used together. Coleman could not hear her instructor because of the wind and the sound of the propeller. She learned how to fly by feeling how her instructor moved the controls. Coleman died in 1926 while performing in an air show. Even in her death, she was a hero to all those who dreamed.

A Dream of Flying

After reading the story, answer the questions.
Fill in the circle next to the correct answer.

1. How did Coleman learn to fly?
   - (a) by learning French
   - (b) by feeling the controls
   - (c) by listening to her instructor
   - (d) by getting a pilot's license on June 15, 1921

2. Which word fits best in the blank? "Joe spoke softly. Bella had to _____ to hear him."
   - (a) strain
   - (b) thrill
   - (c) descent
   - (d) plummet

3. This story is mainly about
   - (a) a dream
   - (b) hard work
   - (c) an aviator
   - (d) flying biplanes

4. What did Coleman do to save herself in the nick of time?
   - (a) she pulled the control stick back
   - (b) she pulled the control stick hard
   - (c) she pulled the control stick to the left
   - (d) she pulled the control stick to the right

5. Think about how the word *pilot* relates to *aviator*. What words relate in the same way?

pilot : aviator

   - (a) engine : cockpit
   - (b) plummet : skyward
   - (c) propeller : control
   - (d) instructor : teacher

Answer Sheets

Student Name: _____

Title of Reading Passage: _____

1. (a) (b) (c) (d)

2. (a) (b) (c) (d)

3. (a) (b) (c) (d)

4. (a) (b) (c) (d)

5. (a) (b) (c) (d)

Student Name: _____

Title of Reading Passage: _____

1. (a) (b) (c) (d)

2. (a) (b) (c) (d)

3. (a) (b) (c) (d)

4. (a) (b) (c) (d)

5. (a) (b) (c) (d)

Bibliography

Alexander, Bryan and Cherry. *What Do We Know About the Inuit?* Peter Bedrick Books, MacDonald Young Books, Ltd., 1995.

Anderson, Dave. *The Story of Basketball.* Morrow Junior Books, William Morrow and Company, Inc., 1988.

Beck, Roger B., Linda Black, Larry S. Krieger, Phillip C. Naylor, and Dahia Ibo Shabaka. *World History: Patterns of Interaction.* McDougal Littell Inc., 2003.

Binns, Tristan Boyer. *The EPA: Environmental Protection Agency.* Heinemann Library, Reed Education & Professional Publishing, 2003.

Bockenhauer, Mark H. and Stephen F. Cunha. *Our Fifty States.* National Geographic Society, 2004.

Chase, Richard. *The Jack Tales.* Houghton Mifflin Company, 1971.

Davis, Kenneth C. *Don't Know Much About Rosa Parks.* HarperCollins Publishers, 2005.

——. *Don't Know Much About the Pioneers.* HarperCollins Publishers, 2003.

Dolan, Graham. *Measuring Time.* Heinemann Library, Reed Educational & Professional Publishing, 2001.

Foster, Ruth. *Take Five Minutes: Fascinating Facts about Geography.* Teacher Created Materials, Inc., 2003.

——. *Take Five Minutes: Fascinating Facts and Stories for Reading and Critical Thinking.* Teacher Created Materials, Inc., 2001.

Fritz, Jean. *You Want Women to Vote, Lizzie Stanton?* G.P. Putnam's Sons, 1995.

Hamilton, Leni. *Clara Barton.* Chelsea House Publishers, Main Line Book Co., 1988.

Hart, Philip S. *Up in the Air: The Story of Bessie Coleman.* Carolrhoda Books, Inc., 1996.

Holub, Joan. *Yankee Doodle Riddles: American History Fun.* Albert Whitman & Company, 2003.

Kastner, Joseph. *John James Audubon.* Harry N. Abrams, Inc., 1992.

Kent, Zachary. *James Cook.* Children's Press, Inc., 1991.

Koslow, Philip. *The Seminole Indians.* Chelsea House Publishers, Main Line Book Co., 1994.

Lubar, Steven, and Kathleen M. Kendrick. *Legacies: Collecting American History at the Smithsonian.* Smithsonian Institution Press, 2001.

Lutz, Norma Jean. *John Paul Jones.* Chelsea House Publishers, Main Line Book Co., 2000.

Meltzer, Milton. *A Book About Names.* Thomas Y. Crowell, 1984.

Merriam Webster's Geographical Dictionary (3rd ed.). Merriam-Webster, Inc., 1997.

Moore, Cathy. *The Daring Escape of Ellen Craft.* Carolrhoda Books Inc., Lerner Publishing Group, 2002.

Patent, Dorothy Hinshaw. *Treasures of the Spanish Main.* Benchmark Books, Marshall Cavendish, 2000.

Perl, Lila. *From Top Hats to Baseball Caps, From Bustles to Blue Jeans: Why We Dress the Way We Do.* Clarion Books, Houghton Mifflin Company, 1990.

Presnall, Judith Janda. *Sled Dogs.* KidHaven Press, Thomson Gale, 2005.

Raabe, Emily. *Buffalo Soldiers and the Western Frontier.* The Rosen Publishing Group, Inc., 2003.

Rozakis, Laurie. *Mathew Henson & Robert Peary: the Race for the North Pole.* Blackbirch Press, Inc., 1994.

Rubel, David. *Mr. President: The Human Side of America's Chief Executives.* Time-Life Books, 1998.

Salkeld, Audrey. *Climbing Everest: Tales of Triumph and Tragedy on the World's Highest Mountain.* National Geographic Society, 2003.

Schwabacher, Martin. *Puerto Rico.* Benchmark Books, Marshall Cavendish, 2001.

Scordato, Ellen. *Sarah Winnemucca: Northern Paiute Warrior and Diplomat.* Chelsea House Publishers, 1992.

Stein, R. Conrad. *Valley Forge.* Children's Press, Inc., 1994.

Stepanchuk, Carol. *Red Eggs and Dragon Boats: Celebrating Chinese Festivals.* Pacific View Press, 1994.

Sutcliffe, Andrea. *The New York Public Library Amazing U.S. Geography: A Book of Answers for Kids.* John Wiley & Sons, Inc., 2001.

Swain, Gwenyth. *President of the Underground Railroad: A Story about Levi Coffin.* Carolrhoda Books, Inc., Lerner Publishing Group, 2001.

Tucker, Tom. *Brainstorm!: The Stories of Twenty American Kid Inventors.* Farrar, Straus, and Giroux, 1995.

Williams, Brian. *Latitude & Longitude.* Smart Apple Media, 2003.

Yancey, Diane. *Life on the Pony Express.* Lucent Books, Inc., 2001.

Young, Robert. *Old Ironsides.* Lerner Publications Company, 2001

Answer Key

Dog Boots
1. c
4. b
2. a
5. d
3. a

Why They Had Wands
1. d
4. d
2. c
5. b
3. c

Reading with One's Fingers
1. d
4. b
2. a
5. a
3. d

Jack and the Two-Headed Giant
1. a
4. a
2. d
5. c
3. d

A Game that Used Peach Baskets
1. a
4. b
2. d
5. c
3. a

On Top of the World
1. c
4. a
2. c
5. b
3. a

How an Observation Helped Train a Horse
1. d
4. d
2. c
5. a
3. a

A Race for the Strong
1. c
4. b
2. b
5. c
3. d

Escape in the Open
1. b
4. c
2. c
5. d
3. d

Record Temperatures
1. b
4. a
2. c
5. a
3. b

Buried Alive
1. b
4. b
2. d
5. d
3. c

Valley Forge
1. d
4. d
2. b
5. b
3. a

Connecting Polygons to Month Names
1. a
4. b
2. b
5. c
3. a

The Painter and His Horse
1. c
4. b
2. d
5. b
3. c

Where Water Glows in the Dark
1. d
4. b
2. d
5. a
3. b

The Moon Festival
1. a
4. d
2. d
5. c
3. b

A Race of Life and Death
1. a
4. d
2. b
5. c
3. d

How Some Nicknames Came About
1. b
4. d
2. b
5. c
3. c

The Toilet-Paper Trail
1. a
4. c
2. b
5. d
3. c

What Stanton Dreaded
1. b
4. d
2. c
5. a
3. b

The Geographic Center
1. d
4. d
2. c
5. c
3. a

A Key to Mongol Horsemanship
1. d
4. a
2. c
5. a
3. c

History Humor
1. c
4. a
2. d
5. b
3. b

"I Have Not Yet Begun to Fight!"
1. c
4. c
2. a
5. d
3. a

John and Jane Doe
1. d
4. c
2. b
5. b
3. d

A Boy with Cold Ears
1. b
4. a
2. a
5. c
3. d

Why Wagons Were Called Ships
1. d
4. a
2. c
5. b
3. c

Who and Where
1. b
4. d
2. c
5. a
3. c

A Time to Wear a Sword
1. c
4. b
2. c
5. d
3. a

When Rivers Catch on Fire
1. a
4. b
2. b
5. c
3. a

The Pony Express
1. b
4. c
2. a
5. d
3. b

Losing a Year for a Day
1. c
4. c
2. b
5. d
3. b

Seven Words
1. d
4. c
2. b
5. a
3. d

Old Ironsides
1. b
4. a
2. b
5. d
3. a

A Palindrome and a President
1. d
4. b
2. c
5. c
3. d

A Stuffed Hero and Ordinary Shoes
1. a
4. c
2. b
5. d
3. b

Buffalo Soldiers
1. d
4. a
2. d
5. b
3. a

Imaginary Lines and the World's Smallest Bird
1. c
4. a
2. a
5. d
3. b

Sunken Treasure
1. c
4. b
2. a
5. d
3. d

What the Numbers Tell
1. d
4. d
2. b
5. c
3. a

Tricked into Eating Salted Cabbage
1. d
4. c
2. c
5. a
3. b

Nurse on the Battlefield
1. c
4. d
2. b
5. b
3. a

Coffin's House
1. c
4. a
2. a
5. c
3. d

A Dream of Flying
1. b
4. a
2. a
5. d
3. c